T0320478

Enhancing Software Fault Prediction With Machine Learning:

Emerging Research and Opportunities

Ekbal Rashid
Aurora's Technological and Research Institute, India

A volume in the Advances in
Systems Analysis, Software
Engineering, and High Performance
Computing (ASASEHPC) Book Series

Published in the United States of America by
    IGI Global
    Engineering Science Reference (an imprint of IGI Global)
    701 E. Chocolate Avenue
    Hershey PA, USA 17033
    Tel: 717-533-8845
    Fax: 717-533-8661
    E-mail: cust@igi-global.com
    Web site: http://www.igi-global.com

Library of Congress Cataloging-in-Publication Data

Names: Rashid, Ekbal, 1976- author.
Title: Enhancing software fault prediction with machine learning : emerging
    research and opportunities / by Ekbal Rashid.
Description: Hershey, PA : Engineering Science Reference, [2018] | Includes
    bibliographical references and index.
Identifiers: LCCN 2017015192| ISBN 9781522531852 (hardcovder) | ISBN
    9781522531869 (ebook)
Subjects: LCSH: Software failures--Prevention--Data processing. | Computer
    software--Quality control--Data processing. | Software maintenance--Data
    processing. | Computer system failures. | Computer software--Reliability.
    | Machine learning.
Classification: LCC QA76.76.F34 R37 2018 | DDC 005.3028/7--dc23 LC record available at
https://lccn.loc.gov/2017015192

This book is published in the IGI Global book series Advances in Systems Analysis, Software
Engineering, and High Performance Computing (ASASEHPC) (ISSN: 2327-3453; eISSN: 2327-
3461)

British Cataloguing in Publication Data
A Cataloguing in Publication record for this book is available from the British Library.

All work contributed to this book is new, previously-unpublished material.
The views expressed in this book are those of the authors, but not necessarily of the publisher.

For electronic access to this publication, please contact: eresources@igi-global.com.

Advances in Systems Analysis, Software Engineering, and High Performance Computing (ASASEHPC) Book Series

ISSN:2327-3453
EISSN:2327-3461

Editor-in-Chief: Vijayan Sugumaran, Oakland University, USA

MISSION

The theory and practice of computing applications and distributed systems has emerged as one of the key areas of research driving innovations in business, engineering, and science. The fields of software engineering, systems analysis, and high performance computing offer a wide range of applications and solutions in solving computational problems for any modern organization.

The **Advances in Systems Analysis, Software Engineering, and High Performance Computing (ASASEHPC) Book Series** brings together research in the areas of distributed computing, systems and software engineering, high performance computing, and service science. This collection of publications is useful for academics, researchers, and practitioners seeking the latest practices and knowledge in this field.

COVERAGE

- Parallel Architectures
- Computer graphics
- Software engineering
- Engineering Environments
- Human-computer interaction
- Enterprise information systems
- Storage Systems
- Performance Modelling
- Distributed Cloud Computing
- Network Management

IGI Global is currently accepting manuscripts for publication within this series. To submit a proposal for a volume in this series, please contact our Acquisition Editors at Acquisitions@igi-global.com or visit: http://www.igi-global.com/publish/.

The Advances in Systems Analysis, Software Engineering, and High Performance Computing (ASASEHPC) Book Series (ISSN 2327-3453) is published by IGI Global, 701 E. Chocolate Avenue, Hershey, PA 17033-1240, USA, www. igi-global.com. This series is composed of titles available for purchase individually; each title is edited to be contextually exclusive from any other title within the series. For pricing and ordering information please visit http://www.igi-global. com/book-series/advances-systems-analysis-software-engineering/73689. Postmaster: Send all address changes to above address. ©© 2018 IGI Global. All rights, including translation in other languages reserved by the publisher. No part of this series may be reproduced or used in any form or by any means – graphics, electronic, or mechanical, including photocopying, recording, taping, or information and retrieval systems – without written permission from the publisher, except for non commercial, educational use, including classroom teaching purposes. The views expressed in this series are those of the authors, but not necessarily of IGI Global.

Titles in this Series

701 East Chocolate Avenue, Hershey, PA 17033, USA
Tel: 717-533-8845 x100 ● Fax: 717-533-8661
E-Mail: cust@igi-global.com ● www.igi-global.com

Table of Contents

Preface

The basic aim of software fault prediction is to identify error prone tasks as the cost can be minimized with advance knowledge about the errors and this early treatment of error will enhance the software quality. Case-based reasoning is used to predict software quality of the system by examining a software module and predicting whether it is faulty or non-faulty. In this book an attempt has been made to propose a model with the help of previous data which is used for prediction. Five different similarity measures, namely, Euclidean, Canberra, Exponential, Clark, and Manhattan are used for retrieving the matching cases from the knowledgebase. The use of different similarity measures to find the best method significantly increases the estimation accuracy and reliability. Based on the research findings in this book it can be concluded that applying similarity measures in case-based reasoning may be a viable technique for software fault prediction. In addition to software fault prediction, this book attempts to develop a system to predict rate of improvement of the software quality at a particular point of time with respect to the number of lines of code present in the software. Having calculated the error level (EL) and degree of excellence (DE) at two points in time, I can move forward towards the estimation of the rate of improvement of the software quality with respect to time. This parameter can be used to judge the amount of effort put into while developing software and can add a new dimension to the understanding of software quality in software engineering domain. The effort of this book is also directed towards introducing a new mathematical model to understand the state of quality of software by calculating parameters such as the time gap and quality gap with relation to some predefined standard software quality or in relation to some chalked out software quality plan. This book also indicates methods to calculate the difference in the quality of the software being developed and the model software which has been decided upon as the criteria for comparison. These methods will provide a better understanding of quality as compared to other standards. The book also presents some new ideas about estimation and evaluation of the quality of software. At the outset, it deals with the possibilities of using a standard conversion method so that lines of code from any language may be compared and be used as a uniform metric. It also attempts to explain in depth the method of evaluating and understanding quality with respect to development time as well as LOC. The present work is also credited through the introduction of some new terms like efficiency and variation to understand the change in software quality. The main focus is to evaluate and estimate software quality at a particular stage of software development. This is not average quality understanding, but quality estimation at a particular instance. One of the salient aspects of the method suggested is that the developer can evaluate the work at any stage using the methods given to review the present status and make future plans to meet the required target. Different types of variations have also been outlined in the book. This book covers the different kinds of graphical shapes that may arise out of possible cases and gives their respective interpretations.

INTRODUCTION

About the Book

The book addresses software quality prediction using machine learning technique such as case-based reasoning. In this research work I have addressed an important problem in the area of software fault prediction using a popular and relatively important methodology known as case-based reasoning. The unique point about this approach that makes it different from other Artificial Intelligence approaches is that in CBR knowledge gained in the form of experiences that makes it easier to gather in contrast to complex domain specific knowledge that are usually in the form of rules. Case-based reasoning (CBR) has grown from a relatively exact and hard to find a research area in a field of extensive interest over the last few years. Activities are rapidly rising - as seen by the increased rate of research papers, availability of commercial products, and also reports on applications in regular use. In Europe, researchers and application developers met at the first European workshop on case-based reasoning, which took place in Germany, November 1993. It gathered around 120 people and more than 80 papers on scientific and application-oriented research were presented (Aamodt & Plaza, 1994). The roots of case-based reasoning lie in artificial intelligence. Artificial Intelligence (AI) is a branch of computer science concerned with the development of intelligent behavior and learning in machines. One of the initial goals was to create machines that could match or exceed human problem-solving abilities. Energetic efforts to achieve this goal began in the 1950's (Turing, 1950) and, while computers may exceed human problem-solving capabilities in many specific tasks, this goal is still a long way off in many problem areas today. In broad terms, case-based reasoning (CBR) is the process of solving new problems based on the solutions of similar past problems (Kolodner, 1993). CBR is a very popular machine learning technique (Rashid, Patnaik, & Bhattacherjee, 2012). It is a branch of AI in which reasoning is based on previous experiences. These experiences are stored as problem-solving instances, called cases (Kolodner, 1983), and generally include a description of the problem faced and of the solution applied and may also include a measure of the success rate of the solution. This approach makes CBR different from other AI approaches which rely on generalized knowledge of a problem domain. An advantage of CBR is that knowledge gained in the form of experiences is often easier to understand and gather than the complex domain specific knowledge that is generally in the form of rules. With the help of the stored cases it is possible to overcome the knowledge elicitation bottleneck that hinders the development of expert systems (Gonzalez & Dankel, 1993). While the quality of the store of cases does control the performance of a CBR system, maintenance of the knowledgebase is one approach that can improve this potential problem. The focus of this research is on the prediction of the reasoner's experiential information source, called the knowledgebase. Prediction of software quality (fault) from the knowledgebase will be made with some specific performance objective in mind.

Major Issues in Case-Based Reasoning

There are many important implementation and research issues associated with case-based reasoning (Aamodt, 1993; Althoff, 2001).

- Reducing the maintenance cost.
- Removing the ambiguous record set from case base or knowledgebase.
- Modification of case base or knowledgebase.

Therefore, making case-based reasoning (CBR), effective and efficient I have introduced some new features, i.e., renovation of the knowledgebase (KBS) and reducing the maintenance cost by removing the ambiguous cases from the KBS. Renovation of knowledgebase is the process of removing duplicate record stored in knowledgebase as well as adding new problems along with new solutions. Five different similarity measures have been used to find the best method that increases the accuracy. The experimental results reveal that the CBR method with the implementation of similarity measures is a viable technique for the fault prediction with practical advantages.

Aim of the Research

Case-based reasoning is used in medical diagnosis, web-based planning as well as in multiagent systems. These are the major application areas of case-based reasoning. Current research on case-based reasoning is going on, but most of the systems are still prototypes and needs to available in the market as a commercial product (Begum et al., 2011). Case-based reasoning is a strong approach to problem solving and learning that has received a lot of attention over the last few years. Originating in the US, the basic idea and fundamental theories have spread to other continents. The 7th International Conference on Case-Based Reasoning was held in Belfast, Northern Ireland, UK, in August 2007 (www.springer.com/computer/ai/book/978-3-540-74138-1). This conference attracted some of the field's leading minds who came to present their findings and discuss the latest developments and applications in the field. Fifteen full length research papers and eighteen poster papers are presented along with three invited talks. The Industrial conference on data mining (ICDM) was also held in New York in the month July 2013 (www.data-mining-forum.de/comments_icdm2013.php). These conferences reflect the growing interest of scientists in this area. Although case-based reasoning is used as a generic term in this chapter, CBR solves problems using the previously stored knowledge, and captures new knowledge, making it instantly available for solving the next problem. Therefore, case-based reasoning can be seen as a method for problem solving, and also as a method to capture new experience and make it immediately available for problem solving. It can be seen as a learning and knowledge-discovery approach, since it can capture from new experience some general knowledge, such as case prototypes, classes and some higher-level concept. The idea of case-based reasoning originally came from the cognitive science community which discovered that people are rather reasoning on formerly successfully solved cases than on general rules. The case-based reasoning community aims to develop computer models that follow this cognitive process. In many application areas, computer models have been successfully developed, which were based on CBR, such as signal/image processing and interpretation tasks, help-desk applications, medical applications and e-commerce product-selling systems. The typical case-based reasoning methods have some characteristics that distinguish them from the other approaches. First, a typical case is usually understood to have a certain degree of richness of information contained in it, and a certain complexity with respect to its internal organization. That is, a feature vector holding some values and a corresponding class is not what we would call a typical case description. What we refer to as typical case-based methods also have another characteristic property. They are able to modify, or adapt, a retrieved solution when applied to a different problem solving context. A paradigmatic case-based method also utilizes general background knowledge - although its richness, degree of explicit representation, and role within the CBR processes varies. Core methods of typical CBR systems borrow a lot of cognitive psychology theories. CBR systems rely on the contents of the various knowledge containers, as these effect how well a system performs. Explicit or implicit changes in the task, the reasoning environment or the user base may all affect the fit between the state of current system knowledge and the task being undertaken. This may affect the performance of the system in terms of its efficiency, competence and solution quality. Over time, the system's knowledge must be updated in order to maintain or improve performance as changes take place. This maintenance should take the form of support tools that monitor a system's state to determine when and how knowledge should be updated in response to specific performance criteria. An increase in experience with the deployment of long term CBR systems has led to recognition within the field that maintenance of existing systems is an essential element of an operational CBR system (Kolodner, 1993). Without any doubt maintenance issues affect all stages of a system's life cycle and, as such, maintenance is increasingly becoming a focus of interest within the CBR research community (Gomes et al., 2003). In theory, knowledge can be held in any of the knowledge containers and a lack of knowledge in one container can be offset by increasing the knowledge in another. However, as the basic philosophy of CBR is to reuse previous experiences the case base should provide the main knowledge source.

Research Objectives

This research sets out to develop models to predict the software quality. This book explores software quality improvement through early prediction of error patterns. It summarizes a variety of techniques for software quality prediction in the domain of software engineering. The aim of this research is to apply the machine learning approaches, such as case-based reasoning (CBR), to predict software quality. CBR is used to predict software quality of the system by discovering an error-prone module. The system predicts the error after accepting the values of certain parameters of the software. The prediction is based on analogy. The objective is to predict the software quality accurately and use the results in future predictions. The novel idea behind this system is that Knowledgebase (KBS) building is an important task in CBR and it can be built based on world new problems along with world new solutions. Second, reducing the maintenance cost by removing the duplicate record set from the KBS. Third, error prediction with the help of similarity functions. Different similarity measures like Euclidian distance, Canberra distance, Exponential distance, Clark distance and Manhattan distance are selected for use in this approach to work to find the best method that increases reliability. I feel that case-based models are particularly useful when it is difficult to define actual rules about a problem domain. For this purpose, a case-based reasoning model has developed and validated it upon student data. In addition to software fault prediction, this book attempts to develop a system to predict rate of improvement of the software quality at a particular point of time with respect to the number of lines of code present in the software. The effort of this book is also directed towards introducing a new mathematical model to understand the state of quality of software by calculating parameters such as the time gap and quality gap with relation to some predefined standard software quality or in relation to some chalked out software quality plan. The book also presents some new ideas about estimation and evaluation of the quality of software. At the outset, it deals with the possibilities of using a standard conversion method so that lines of code from any language may be compared and be used as a uniform metric.

Specifically, four research objectives were addressed:

1. To develop a technique to model for Software Quality Prediction with Similarity Measures: As an Expert System (Rashid, Patnaik, & Bhattacherjee, 2014a, 2014b, 2014c).
2. To develop a new mathematical model to understand the state of quality of software by calculating parameters such as the time gap and quality gap with relation to some predefined standard software quality (Rashid, Patnaik, & Bhattacherjee, 2013a).
3. To develop a system to predict rate of improvement of the software quality at a particular point of time with respect to the number of lines of code present in the software (Rashid, Patnaik, & Bhattacherjee, 2014d).

4. To develop a model for Estimation and evaluation of change in software quality at a particular stage of software development (Rashid, Patnaik, & Bhattacherjee, 2013b).

Organization of the Book

This book includes seven chapters that are organized as follows:

- Chapter 1 takes a closer look about software quality.
- Chapter 2 presents the literature survey and scope of the present work.
- Chapter 3 focuses on various machine learning approaches in software engineering.
- Chapter 4 describes the methods of software quality prediction with similarity measures: As an Expert System. It advocates the use of case-based reasoning (i.e., CBR) to build a software quality prediction system with the help of human experts.
- Chapter 5 presents the prediction of error level and degree of excellence at a particular stage of development of the software. This chapter explores an attempt to develop a system to predict rate of improvement of the software quality at a particular point of time with respect to the number of lines of code present in the software.
- Chapter 6 introduces the understanding of state of quality of software on the basis of the time gap, quality gap and the difference with the standard model. The chapter suggests methods to calculate the difference in the quality of the software being developed and the model software which has been decided upon as the criteria for comparison.
- Chapter 7 presents the estimation and evaluation of software quality at a particular stage of software development. This chapter suggests a method of comparing the actual rate of software development with the projected or targeted rate. A working function may be devised from past experiences and results. On the basis of the results of comparisons made in this manner, decisions can be taken to improve the quality by increasing the quantity or quality of manpower in order to achieve the quality target within the stipulated time.

The final section presents the conclusion and future work of the book.

REFERENCES

Aamodt, A. (1993) Explanation-driven retrieval, reuse, and learning of cases. *Proceedings of the First European Workshop on Case-Based Reasoning EWCBR-93*, 279-284.

Aamodt, A., & Plaza, E. (1994). Case-Based Reasoning: Foundational Issues, Methodological Variations, and System Approaches. *AI Communications*, *7*(1), 39–59.

Althoff, K.-D. (2001). Case-Based Reasoning. In *Handbook on Software Engineering and Knowledge Engineering* (pp. 549–588). World Scientific.

Begum, S., Ahmed, M. U., Funk, P., Xiong, N., & Folke, M. (2011). Case-Based Reasoning Systems in the Health Sciences: A Survey of Recent Trends and Developments. *IEEE Transactions on Systems, Man and Cybernetics. Part C, Applications and Reviews*, *41*(4), 421–434. doi:10.1109/TSMCC.2010.2071862

Dwadera, R. (2013). *Comments from participants of ICDM*. Retrieved 5 February 2014 from www.data-mining-forum.de/comments_icdm2013.php

Gomes, P., Pereira, F. C., Paiva, P., Seco, N., Carreiro, P., Ferreira, J. L., & Bento, C. (2003). Evaluation of case-based maintenance strategies in software design. *Proceedings of the 5th International Conference on Case-Based Reasoning (ICCBR)*, *2689*, 186–200. doi:10.1007/3-540-45006-8_17

Gonzalez, A., & Dankel, D. (1993). *The Engineering of Knowledge-Based Systems: Theory and Practice*. Englewood Cliffs, NJ: Prentice-Hall.

Kolodner, J. (1983). Reconstructive memory: A computer model. *Cognitive Science*, *7*(4), 281–328. doi:10.1207/s15516709cog0704_2

Kolodner, J. (1993). *Case-Based Reasoning*. San Mateo, CA: Morgan Kaufmann.

Kolodner, J. (1993). *Case-Based Reasoning*. San Mateo, CA: Morgan Kaufmann. doi:10.1016/B978-1-55860-237-3.50005-4

Rashid, E., & Patnaik, S., & Bhattacherjee, V. (2014a). Search-Based Information Retrieval and Fault prediction with distance functions. *International Journal of Software Engineering and its Applications*, *8*(2), 75-86. doi:10.14257/ijseia.8.2.08

Rashid, E., Patnaik, S., & Bhattacherjee, V. (2012). A Survey in the Area of Machine Learning and Its Application for Software Quality Prediction. *Software Engineering Notes, 37*(5). doi:10.1145/2347696.2347709

Rashid, E., Patnaik, S., & Bhattacherjee, V. (2013a). Understanding the State of Quality of Software on the basis of Time Gap, Quality Gap and Difference with Standard Model. *IACSIT International Journal of Engineering and Technology, 5*(3), 2821–2827.

Rashid, E., Patnaik, S., & Bhattacherjee, V. (2013b). Estimation and evaluation of change in software quality at a particular stage of software development. *Indian Journal of Science and Technology, 6*(10).

Rashid, E., Patnaik, S., & Bhattacherjee, V. (2014b). Machine Learning and Software Quality Prediction: As an Expert System. *International Journal of Information Engineering and Electronic Business, 6*(2), 9–27. doi:10.5815/ ijieeb

Rashid, E., Patnaik, S., & Bhattacherjee, V. (2014c). Machine Learning and its application in Software fault prediction with similarity measures. *Proceedings of the 5th International Conference on Computational Vision and Robotic (ICCVR)*. Bhubaneswar, India. Springer.

Rashid, E., Patnaik, S., & Bhattacherjee, V. (2014d). Prediction of rate of Improvement of Software Quality and Development Effort on the Basis of Degree of Excellence with respect to Number of Lines of Code. *International Journal of Computer Engineering and Applications, 5*(3), 6–13.

Turing, A. (1950). Computing machinery and intelligence. *Mind, 59*(236), 433–460. doi:10.1093/mind/LIX.236.433

Weber, R. O., & Richter, M. M. (2007). *Case-based reasoning research and development*. Springer. Retrieve 18 July 2014 from www.springer.com/ computer/ai/book/978-3-540-74138-1

Chapter 1
Software Quality

ABSTRACT

The basic aim of software quality (fault) is to identify error prone tasks as the cost can be minimized with advance knowledge about the errors and this early treatment of error will enhance the software quality. Today quality is critical for survival and success. Customers demand it. Software is now a global business and organizations will not succeed in this global market unless they produce quality products/services and unless the organizations are also perceived by customers to produce quality products and services. I need measures of the characteristics and quality parameters of the development process and its stages, as well as metrics and models to ensure that the development process is under control and moving toward the product's quality objectives.

INTRODUCTION

Since quality is the first step for improvement in anything, to achieve an improved state of affairs, quality must be precisely defined and appropriately measured. But very often in quality engineering and management, the term quality is misunderstood on account of its ambiguous characteristics. The ambiguity aspect of quality owes its origin from the following (Kan, 2012);

- Quality being multi-dimensional with dimensions of entity of interest, the viewpoint on that entity and the quality attributes of that entity gets interpreted differently depending upon the situation and interpreter.

DOI: 10.4018/978-1-5225-3185-2.ch001

- On the basis of conceptualizing quality, it may be referred either in its broadest sense or in its precise connotation.
- Being an element of our everyday language, quality may be interpreted differently depending upon the uses – popular or professional.

However, as the focus of this book will be around the quality of software which is a sort of the professional use of the concept quality as against the popular use of the same, the third point mentioned above duly makes it very clear how quality in popular view is quite different from quality in professional view and hence it draws our attention to take care.

QUALITY IN POPULAR CONNOTATION

Quality in popular connotation highlights the ordinal dimension of the concept discarding the cardinal one, as per which;

- Quality is an elusive attribute that can be felt, talked about and compared but cannot be quantified or measured.
- Quality means opulence, class and taste, i.e., expensive, elaborate and more complex.

In the former sense, if I use two different brands of a product or service, I can feel which one is better, but I won't be possible to express by how much one is better or worse than the other. In fact, under this viewpoint, psychological inclination will be there towards one brand among a group of brands depending upon the liking of the user towards that particular brand. Thus, this assessment will be subjective as it varies from person to person. Accordingly, generalizing whether a brand is qualitative or not is exceedingly tough and rewarding the brand as per the quality is rather tougher. In the latter sense, quality is limited to an undersized group of elegant products or services with sophisticated functionality and items that have a touch of class.

QUALITY IN PROFESSIONAL CONNOTATION

Quality in popular connotation, as I experience, invites delusion and imprecision. Still quality has been and is being treated as the focal point for any firm to have an edge over other competitors. However, the fallacies of the popular connotation of quality no way help the quality up-gradation efforts in the industries. In fact, to develop strategic quality improvement efforts for the betterment of the organizations, quality must be defined in a very professional way. To that extent, the definitions given by Crosby (1979), and Juran and Gryna (1970) seem to be appropriate and hence being used by many quality professionals. While Crosby defines quality as 'conformance to requirements' Juran and Gryna defines it as 'fitness for use.'

Both the definitions give importance to customers' requirements and expectations. While Crosby's view point clusters around the producer's assessment of consumers' requirements and developing the product or service accordingly, the view point of Juran and Gryna focus on consumers' assessment of performance of the product or service. Thus, it is very essential to develop a product or service exactly in line with the customers' requirements and modify if required in further phases analyzing the post-purchase reaction of the customers. From Customers' view point quality is the perceived value of the product or service. In fact, before purchasing a product or service, a customer has a perceived value on that. After purchasing that he/she may derive a level of satisfaction which may be exactly the same as his/her perceived value or more or less. If the realized value happens to be the same as the perceived value, the customer does not find any gap or the producer does not allow finding a gap. That leads to tag the product a quality product. Contrary to this, if the realized value happens to be more than the perceived value, the customer becomes over satisfied and becomes addicted to that brand of the product or service. In such a situation, he/she may refer his/her relatives and friends in favor of the product or service. Accordingly, the performance of that product or service will get due recognition in the market. If the realized value happens to be less than the perceived value, not only the concerned customer will be unhappy, but due to bad word of mouth the market performance of the product or service will also be affected.

While customer buys a product or service he/she compares the assurances given by the producer with his/her expectations for that product or service. In fact, the sale of product depends upon the level of assurances for the quality and the extent to which the assurances are meeting the expectations of the customers. Thus, the customers can appropriately say about the quality of any product or service. To perform well in the market and maintain sustainability pertaining to the market share a product or service has to go for marketing research at development stage to know the customers' expectations or requirements and on post-purchase stage to know the reaction of the customers after using a product or service. The research findings of these researches will help the producer to produce quality output and make necessary changes in the subsequent phases of production depending upon the customers' reactions. This way of producing quality product or service and maintaining the same in the long run will also be applicable to software products.

THE ROLE OF END USERS AND PRIME CUSTOMER

The role of customers and end users is very important in determining the quality parameters of a product. The end-user might define quality as something which is user-friendly and bug-free. If the customer is in perfect position to tell about his expectations and requirements for a product, then it becomes easier to define the quality parameters of that product in quantitative terms. On the other hand, if the customer is not specific about the requirements (mainly in the case of a software product) the quality parameters may remain vague. The role of the customer, as it relates to quality, can never be overstated. From a customer's point of view, quality is the customer's perceived value of the product he or she has purchased, based on a variety of variables such as price, performance, reliability, and satisfaction. The customers are in a perfect position to tell you about the quality, because that's all they're really buying. They're not buying a product. They're buying the assurances that their expectations for that product will be met. And you haven't really got anything else to sell them, but those assurances and quality. From a concept's high-level definition to a product's operational definition, many steps are involved, each of which may be vulnerable to the shortcomings. For example, to achieve the state of conformance to requirements, the customers' requirements must be first gathered and analyzed, specifications to meet those requirements must be produced, and the product must be developed and manufactured accordingly. In each phase of the process, errors can occur that will affect the quality of the finished product. The requirements may be erroneous (this is especially the case for software development), the development and manufacturing process may be subject to variables that induce defects, and so forth. From the customer's perspective, satisfaction after the purchase of the product is the ultimate validation that the product conforms to the requirements and is fit to use. From the producer's perspective, once requirements are specified, developing and producing the product in accordance with the specifications is the path to achieving quality. Usually, for product quality, the lack of defects and good reliability are the most basic measures. Because of the two perspectives on quality (customer satisfaction as the ultimate validation of

4

quality and producer's adherence to requirements to achieve quality), the de facto definition of quality consists of two levels. The first is the intrinsic product quality, often operationally limited to the product defect rate and reliability. This narrow definition is referred to as the "small q" (q for quality). The broader definition of quality includes product quality, process quality, and customer satisfaction, and it is referred to as the "big Q." This two-level approach to the definition of quality is being used in many industries, including the automobile industry, the computer industry (both software and hardware), and the consumer electronics industry (Kan, 2012).

WHAT IS SOFTWARE QUALITY?

Software quality is defined as the quality that ensures customer satisfaction by offering all the customer deliverables on performance, standards and ease of operations (Jawadekar, 2006). Software quality can also be defined as conformance to explicitly stated and implicitly stated functional requirements. The explicitly stated functional requirements can be derived from the requirements stated by the customer which are generally documented in some form. However, implicit requirements are requirements which are not stated explicitly but are intended. In software, the simple sense of product quality is commonly known as a free from "bugs" in the product. It is also the most basic sense of conformance to requirements, because if the software contains too many functional faults, the basic requirement of providing the desired function is not met. This definition is usually expressed in two ways: defect rate (e.g., number of defects per million lines of source code, per function point, or other unit) and reliability (e.g., number of failures per n hours of operation, mean time to failure, or the probability of failure-free operation at a specified time). Customer satisfaction is usually measured by percent satisfied or unsatisfied (neutral and dissatisfied) from customer satisfaction surveys. To reduce bias, techniques such as blind surveys (the interviewer does not know the customer and the customer does not know the company the interviewer represents) are usually used. In addition to overall customer satisfaction with the software product, satisfaction towards specific attributes is also gauged. For example, the higher the functional complexity of the software, the harder it becomes to achieve maintainability. Depending on the type of software and customers, different weighting factors are needed for different quality attributes. For large customers with sophisticated networks and real-time processing, performance and reliability may be the most important attributes. For customers with standalone systems and simple operations, on the other hand, ease of use, installability, and documentation may be more important. In view of these discussions, the updated definition of quality (i.e., conformance to customers' requirements) is especially relevant to the software industry. It is not surprising that requirements errors constitute one of the major problem categories in software development.

DESCRIPTION OF SOFTWARE QUALITY ATTRIBUTES AND SOFTWARE INTERNAL ATTRIBUTES

External Factors of Software

It is known to all, quality is an important concept that is "tough to define", impossible to evaluate, easy to recognize. In order to define such a concept, a lot of research has been done. At last, a number of quality attributes (also known as quality characteristics, quality factors or quality criteria) are defined to describe the quality (Kitchenham, 1990; Guceglioglu & Demirors, 2005; Svahnberg & Wohlin, 2005; Anderson & John, 2005). The ISO 9126 standard for information technology provides a framework for the evaluation of software quality, which defines six product quality characteristics, i.e., portability, maintainability, functionality, reliability, usability, efficiency (International Organization for Standardization. (2003)). Software quality attributes are also called as non-functional requirements in the software engineering domain. Different customers pay particular attention to different software quality attributes for different reasons. It should be emphasized that the quality of exact software holds the stability of its success in the software market. If the system can satisfy all the functional requirements, e.g., an ATM machine can issue the correct amount of money that customer asks to withdraw, but fails to satisfy because the response time is too long, then the software system will hardly be considered as a good one and the customer is unlikely to accept the system. This issue is even more crucial for information systems.

Internal Factors of Software

Software can be seen as an entity in a sequence of internal attributes, such as size, structure, complexity and so on, which are capable of relating the internal structure and character of the software accurately and widely to a considerable extent. For the use of being appropriate and comprehensive, metrics are introduced to standardize and measure the internal attributes.

CONCLUSION

The aim of software quality is elusive in an actual project environment. The measures differ from project to project and organization to organization. Criteria vary as a function of the specific characteristics of the project, the need of the users and stakeholders, and the application requirement of the system and software. Today quality is critical for survival and success. Customers demand it. Software is now a global business and organizations will not succeed in this global market unless they produce quality products/services and unless the organizations are also perceived by customers to produce quality products and services. It applies as much software development and support as to any other product or service. To improve quality during development, I need models of the development process, and within the process, I need to select and deploy specific methods and approaches, and employ proper tools and technologies. I need measures of the characteristics and quality parameters of the development process and its stages, as well as metrics and models to ensure that the development process is under control and moving toward the product's quality objectives.

REFERENCES

Anderson, J., & John, L. (2005). How to produce better quality test software. *IEEE Instrumentation & Measurement Magazine*, 8(3), 34–38. doi:10.1109/MIM.2005.1502445

Guceglioglu, A. S., & Demirors, O. (2005). Using Software Quality Characteristics to Measure Business Process Quality. *Proceedings of the 3rd International Conference on Business Process management*, 374-379.

International Organization for Standardization. (2003). *ISO/IEC 9126: Information Technology Software Product Evaluation Quality Characteristics and Guidelines for their Use*. Author.

Jawadekar, W. S. (2006). *Software Engineering principles and practice* (1st ed.). New Delhi, India: Tata McGraw-Hill.

Kan, S.H. (2012). Metrics and Models in Software Quality Engineering (2nd ed.). Pearson.

Kitchenham, B. (1990). *Software Metrics in Software Reliability Handbook.* New York: Elsevier Applied Science.

Svahnberg, M., & Wohlin, C. (2005). An investigation of a method for identifying a software architecture candidate with respect to quality attributes. *Empirical Software Engineering, 10*(2), 149–181. doi:10.1007/s10664-004-6190-y

Chapter 2
Literature Survey and Scope of the Present Work

ABSTRACT

As I know large numbers of techniques and models have already been worked out in the area of error estimation. Identifying and locating errors in software projects is a complicated job. Particularly, when project sizes grow. This chapter enlists and reviews existing work to predict the quality of the software using various machine learning techniques. In this chapter key finding from prior studies in the field of software fault prediction has been discussed. Various advantages and disadvantages of the methods used for software quality prediction, have been explained in a detail. What are the problems solved are also mentioned in this section. Description of earlier research work and present research work has summarized in one place.

INTRODUCTION

Software quality (fault) prediction is a challenging task. Wide research has been done in this direction. Prediction models based on software metrics can predict the number of errors in software modules. Timely predictions of such models can be used to direct quality improvement, cost effectiveness etc. It also explains the scope of the present work.

DOI: 10.4018/978-1-5225-3185-2.ch002

LITERATURE SURVEY

Zhang and Tsai (2002) mention that machine learning methods are used to predict or estimate software quality, software size, software development cost, project or software effort etc. Machine learning algorithms have proven to be of great practical value in a variety of applications. The field of software engineering turns out to be a fertile ground where many software development and maintenance tasks could be formulated as learning problems and approached in terms of learning algorithms. In this work, they have discussed issues and current status regarding machine learning applications to software engineering problems. They considered machine learning methods that can be used to complement existing software tools. The strength of machine learning methods lies in the fact that they have sound mathematical and logical justifications and can be used to create and compile verifiable knowledge about the design and development of software artifacts (Zhang & Tsai, 2002). Mertik et al. (2006) presented the use of advanced tool for data mining called multimethod on the case of building software fault prediction model. Current software quality estimation models often involve use of data mining and machine learning techniques for building a software fault prediction model. In this work, they have presented some of the methods integrated within the multimethod data mining tool. They have introduced the multimethod data mining tool which was developed in the laboratory for the system design in University of Maribor (Lenic, n.d.), and it was presented as a case study of building the fault prediction model based on the data from the metrics data program data repository (Lenic, n.d.). In their study, they adapted and combined some single methods, approaches with the multimethod tool on the real data sets from the MDP data repository, where they got promising results. They have given an overview of some efficient single methods approach for support of multi-methods. These are decision tree (DT), support vector machine (SVM) and genetic algorithm (GA). With multi-method tools, they have generated four different fault prediction models. Each model has been built with the different techniques. In every experiment, they sampled the accuracy on learning set and test as also the size of the generated model/ classifier. In this work, they have presented the advanced data mining tool multimethod for building software fault prediction models. They showed the use of the tool on three different datasets of the NASA IV & V Metrics data program project and using multimethod tool they got quite better results as with standard supervised machine learning methods for building such prediction models. Therefore, the reasons for which multimethod approach was appropriate for building the software fault prediction models are:

1. It provides reasoning based knowledge in the form of a multimethod tree.
2. It combines different single methods for building fault prediction software model.

Challagulla (2006) proposed a framework that provides a flexible and effective environment for mission-critical software defect prediction using the Memory-Based Reasoning (MBR) method. The framework guided the user through the logical process of selecting the appropriate MBR configuration that gave the best prediction depending on the software defect data. The framework was constructed using real-time defect data sets obtained from NASA's MDP data repository. The real-time defect data sets were used in this work. Memory-based reasoning technique (Stanfill & Watlz, 1986; Waltz, 1987) is one such quantitative method that predicts a new case by retrieving similar cases from the past. It uses the past cases to predict the solution to the current problem. If necessary, it revises the proposed solution and saves it to form a new case. The various steps described the memory-based learning process (Kasif et al., 1995). As observed, there were many independent configuration parameters that influence the prediction capabilities of the memory-based reasoning classification method. Any memory-based reasoning data analysis should begin with some default values for the number of nearest neighbors, combination function, weighted function and distance metric. These parameters will be incrementally tuned on the basis of the results obtained as they evolved through building the framework. They assumed that all the attributes were weighted equally and the combination function assigns a weight to nearest neighbors by their distances, with weights decreasing as the distance of the neighbor increases from the target. A preliminary observation was that using raw defect data with no weighting function and data pre-processing, the standard Euclidean measure was a good choice for software defect data prediction. They noticed that as the number of nearest neighbors increases the accuracy also increased. Gupta, Goyal and Harish (2011) addressed software quality as the degree to which software possesses a desired combination of attributes such as reliability, maintainability, efficiency, portability, usability and reusability. A software quality model allows the software development team to track & detect potential software defects. A number of software quality models were used to build quality software in the industry. The aim of building a new model was to predict the fault labels of the model for further release of the software. The term quality model was defined in (ISO/IEC 14598, 1999) as the set of characteristics and relationship between them. Quality models can be divided into two categories based on the approach which has used to build those as given in (Fenton & Pfleeger, 1997).

• Fixed-Model Approach

It was assumed that all important quality factors needed to monitor a project where a subset of those was a published model.

• "Define-Your-Own-Model" Approach

They accepted the general philosophy that quality was composed of many attributes, but they met with prospective users to reach a consensus on which quality attributes were important for a given product.

Together it was decided on a decomposition in which they agreed to the specific relationship between them. Boehm and McCall models are typical examples of the fixed quality model. Trendowicz and Punter (2003), have done an excellent survey of different approaches of modeling quality. A software quality model is a useful tool towards achieving the objectives of a software quality assurance initiative. A software quality estimation model allows the software development team to track and detect potential software defects relatively early during the development which is critical to many high assurance systems. According to Khoshgoftaar (Khoshgoftaar, Cukic, & Seliya, 2002) has described six software quality estimation techniques, namely Regression Tree (RT), Fuzzy Systems (FS), Case-Based Reasoning (CBR), Rule-Based Systems (RBS), Multiple Linear Regression (MLR) and Neural Networks (NN). In this work they have studied that various techniques have been developed for software quality estimation, most of which are suited either for prediction or for classification but not for both. They discussed the issues in software quality estimation. Various techniques were needed to discover faults earlier in the development of software statistical models.

After studying existing quality modeling techniques, they concluded that no single quality model copes with all of their requirements, but a combined use of techniques resulted in effective problem solving in comparison with each technology used individually and exclusively such as fuzzy and rule based system. Zhong, Khoshgoftaar, and Seliya (2004) proposed the use of unsupervised learning (i.e., clustering) techniques to build a software quality estimation with the help of a software engineering human expert. Current software quality estimation models often involve the use of supervised learning methods to train a software quality classifier or a software fault prediction model. In such models, the dependent variable was a software quality measurement indicating the quality of a software module by either a risk-based class membership or the number of faults, such a measurement may be inaccurate or even unavailable. In such situations, the use of unsupervised learning techniques to build a software quality estimation system with the help of a software engineering human experts, clustering and expert-based software quality estimation is an interactive process.

Such an approach was important for software projects where resources were relatively limited and finite. The expert specifies other statistics from the software measurement dataset needed to accurately label each other as either fault prone or not fault prone. The clustering analyst was a professional specializing in data mining and machine learning techniques while the labeling expert was a professional with over fifteen years of experience in software quality and reliability engineering. Challagulla, Bastani, and Yen (2005), proposed a variety of software defect prediction techniques, but none has proven to be consistently accurate. Those techniques include statistical methods, machine learning methods, parametric models and mixed algorithm. This work provides a critical review of software defect prediction techniques with special emphasis on machine learning based methods. These techniques were applied to three real-time defect data sets obtained from NASA's MDP data repository. All defects frequently exhibited non-normal characteristics such as skewness, unstable variances, collinearity and excessive outliers (Pickard, Kitchenham, & Linkman, 1999).

Statistical, machine learning and mixed techniques were widely used to predict software defects. In this work, they evaluated empirically the accuracy of predicting the number of defects using machine learning and statistical prediction systems. They used 70% of the data as training data and 30% as the test data. Their input attributes were treated as continuous values, while the output discrete or continuous values depending on the classifier were used. Shepperd and Kododa (2001) used simulation to compare software prediction using stepwise regression, rule induction, case-based reasoning (CBR), and artificial neural networks (ANN). Mair et al. (2000) investigated the prediction models on real software data. They compared these techniques in terms of accuracy, explanatory value, and configurability. Emam et al. (2001) compared different case-based reasoning classifiers and concluded that there was no added advantage in varying the combination of parameters.

Whilst Watson and Marir (1994) identified a number of additional adaptation strategies, *k*-NN and rule based approaches are the most popular. Hanney and Keane (1997) described an interesting alternative, which learns how to adapt by comparing feature differences and solution differences. More works such as Althoff (2001), Bergmann (2002), and for a comparison of different approaches, to the paper by Finnie and Sun (2003). It has long been recognized that a major contribution to successful software engineering is the ability to be able to make effective predictions particularly in the realms of costs and quality. Consequently, there has been significant research activity in this area, much of which has focused on effort and defect prediction. Both these problems are characterised by an absence of theory, inconsistency and uncertainty that make them well suited to CBR approaches. It was suggested in the early 1980s that analogy might form a good basis for software project effort prediction (Boehm, 1981). An early contribution was by Maiden and Sutcliffe (Mair et al., 2000; Maiden, 1991) who suggested that analogical reasoning techniques might be employed to support the reuse of software specifications. This was achieved by mapping both the target and source (case-base) requirements specification descriptions into more abstract representations to facilitate the measurement of similarity. (Khoshgoftaar, Bullard, & Gao, 2003) several studies have shown that the accuracy of models improves when outliers and data noise are removed from the training data set.

Khoshgoftaar and Gao (2007) identified which software modules are likely to be faulty is an effective technique for enhancing software quality. Khan et al. (2006) compared and discussed about software quality prediction approaches based on case-based reasoning, fuzzy logic, neural networks, support vector machine, expectation maximum likelihood algorithm and Bayesian belief network. In this study gives better comparative insight about these approaches, and helps to select an approach based on available resources and desired level of quality.

SCOPE OF THE PRESENT WORK

As I know the software fault prediction is one of the most interesting research areas in the domain of software engineering for last few decades. Large numbers of techniques and models have already been worked out in the area of error estimation. Identifying and locating errors in software projects is a complicated job. Particularly, when project sizes grow. The aim of this research work on software quality estimation is to identify error prone tasks as the cost can be minimized with advance knowledge about the errors and this early treatment of error will enhance the software quality. The objective of this research is to apply the machine learning approaches, such as case-based reasoning, to predict software quality. The system predicts the error after accepting the values of certain parameters of the software. It advocates the use of case-based reasoning (i.e., CBR) to build a software quality prediction system with the help of human experts. The proposed prediction system is a novel approach in the software quality (fault) prediction domain. Like every software system this system also guarantees results oriented future extensions that will make this system a widely-used prediction system in quality estimation.

The popularity and acceptability solely rely on the accuracy of the results given by the system. In this book five similarity measures, namely Euclidean method, Canberra method, Clark method, Exponential method and Manhattan method have been used. For their efficacy in determining errors, the low error programs detected by these methods may help to design error free programs. The software is a console based application and thus does not use the GUI functions of the Operating System, which makes it very fast in execution. This research work introduces the rate of improvement of quality of software largely depends on the development time. This development time is chiefly calculated in clock hours. However, development time does not reflect the effort put in by the developer. A better parameter can be the rate of improvement of quality level or the rate of improvement of the degree of excellence with respect to time. Now this parameter needs the prediction of error level and degree of excellence at a particular stage of development of the software. The book presents a model to understand the state of quality of software by calculating parameters such as the time gap and quality gap. This book also suggests a method of comparing the actual rate of software development with the projected or targeted rate. A working function may be devised from past experiences and results. This working function would give the projected or the expected rate of software development. Then, using the methods given, the actual rate of software development can be calculated at a particular stage of work and the required comparisons can be made. On the basis of the results of comparisons made in this manner, decisions can be taken to improve the quality by increasing the quantity or quality of manpower in order to achieve the quality target within the stipulated time.

REFERENCES

Althoff, K. D. (2001). Case-Based Reasoning. In S. K. Chang (Ed.), *Handbook on Software Engineering and Knowledge Engineering* (pp. 549–588). World Scientific.

Bergmann, R. (2002). *Experience Management - Foundations, Development Methodology, and Internet-Based Applications, LNAI (Vol. 2432)*. Berlin: Springer Verlag.

Boehm, B. W. (1981). *Software Engineering Economics*. Englewood Cliffs, NJ: Prentice-Hall.

Challagulla, V. U., Bastani, F. B., & Yen, I. L. (2006). A Unified Framework for Defect data analysis using the MBR technique. *Proceeding of the 18th IEEE International Conference on Tools with Artificial Intelligence (ICTAI)*.

Challagulla, V. U., Bastani, F. B., Yen, I. L., & Paul, R. A. (2005). Empirical Assessment of Machine Learning based Software Defect Prediction Techniques. *Proceedings of the 10th IEEE International Workshop on Object-Oriented Real-Time Dependable Systems (WORDS)*.

Eman, K., Benlarbi, S., Goel, N., & Rai, S. (2001). Comparing case-based reasoning classifiers for predicting high risk software components. *Journal of Systems Software, Volume, 55*(, 301–310. doi:10.1016/S0164-1212(00)00079-0

Fenton, N. E., & Pfleeger, S. L. (1997). *Software Metrics: A rigorous and practical approach*. Boston: PWS Publishing Company.

Finnie, G. R., & Sun, Z. (2003). R5 model for case-based reasoning. *Knowledge-Based Systems, 16*(1), 59–65. doi:10.1016/S0950-7051(02)00053-9

Gupta, D., Goyal, V. K., & Mittal, H. (2011). Comparative study of soft computing techniques for software quality model. *International Journal of Software Engineering Research & Practices, 1*(1), 33–37.

Hanney, K., & Keane, M. T. (1997). The adaptation knowledge bottleneck: how to ease it by learning from cases. *Proceedings of the 2nd Intl. CBR Conf.*, 359-370. doi:10.1007/3-540-63233-6_506

ISO/IEC 14598. (1999). *International standard, Standard for Information Technology- Software Product Evaluation - Part 1: General Overview*. ISO.

Kasif, S., Salzberg, S., Waltz, D., Rachlin, J., & Aha, D. (1995). *Towards a Framework for Memory-Based Reasoning* (Technical Report 95-132). NECI.

Khan, M. J., Shamail, S., Awais, M. M., & Hussain, T. (2006) Comparative study of various artificial intelligence techniques to predict software quality. *Proceedings of the 10th IEEE multitopic conference INMIC*, 173-177. doi:10.1109/INMIC.2006.358157

Khoshgoftaar, T. M., Bullard, L. A., & Gao, K. (2003). Detecting outlier using Rule-Based modeling for Improving CBR-Based software quality classification models. In Case-Based Reasoning Research and Development (pp. 216-230). Springer-Verlag.

Khoshgoftaar, T. M., Cukic, B., & Seliya, N. (2002). Comparative Study of the Impact of Underlying Models on Module-Order Model Performances. *Proceedings of the 8th IEEE International Symposium on Software Metrics*. doi:10.1109/METRIC.2002.1011335

Khoshgoftaar, T. M., & Gao, K. (2007). Count Models for Software Quality Estimation. *IEEE Transactions on Reliability*, 56(2), 212–222. doi:10.1109/TR.2007.896757

Lenic, M. (n.d.). *Multimetodnagradnjaklasifikacijskihsistemov* (PhD). Maribor.

Maiden, N. A. (1991). Analogy as a paradigm for specification reuse. *Software Engineering Journal*, 6(1), 3–15. doi:10.1049/sej.1991.0001

Mair, C., Kadoda, G., Leflel, M., Phapl, L., Schofield, K., Shepperd, M., & Webster, S. (2000). An Investigation of Machine Learning Based Prediction Systems. *Journal of Systems Software, Volume*, 53(1), 23–29. doi:10.1016/S0164-1212(00)00005-4

Mair, C., Kadoda, G., Leflel, M., Phapl, L., Schofield, K., Shepperd, M., & Webster, S. (2000). An Investigation of Machine Learning Based Prediction Systems. *Journal of Systems Software, 53*(1), 23–29. doi:10.1016/S0164-1212(00)00005-4

Mertik, M., Lenic, M., Stiglic, G., & Kokol, P. (2006). Estimating software quality with advanced data mining techniques. *Proceedings of the International Conference on software Engineering Advances (ICSEA)*.

Pickard, L., Kitchenham, B., & Linkman, S. (1999). An Investigation of Analysis Techniques for Software Datasets. *Proceedings of the Software Metrics Symposium. Proceedings. Sixth International*, 130-142. doi:10.1109/METRIC.1999.809734

Shepperd, M., & Kadoda, G. (2001). Comparing software prediction techniques using simulation. *IEEE Transactions on Software Engineering*, *27*(11), 1014–1022. doi:10.1109/32.965341

Stanfill, C., & Waltz, D. (1986). Towards memory-based reasoning. *Communications of the ACM*, *29*(12), 1213–1228.

Trendowicz, A., & Punter, T. (2003). Quality Modeling for Software Product Lines. *Proceedings of the 7th ECOOP Workshop on Quantitative Approaches in Object-Oriented Software Engineering*.

Waltz, D. L. (1987). Applications of the connection machine. *IEEE Computer Society*, *20*(1), 85–97. doi:10.1109/MC.1987.1663362

Watson, I., & Marir, F. (1994). Case-Based Reasoning: A Review. *The Knowledge Engineering Review*, *9*(4), 327–354. doi:10.1017/S0269888900007098

Zhang, D., & Tsai, J. J. P. (2002). *Machine learning and software engineering* (Technical report TR-1). Department of Computer Science, California State University, Sacramento, CA.

Zhang, D., & Tsai, J. J. (2002). Machine Learning and Software Engineering. *Proceeding of the 14th IEEE International Conference on Tools with Artificial Intelligence (ICTAI)*.

Zhong, S., Khoshgoftaar, T. M., & Seliya, N. (2004). Unsupervised Learning for Expert-Based Software Quality Estimation. *Proceeding of the Eighth IEEE International Symposium on High Assurance Systems Engineering (HASE)*.

Chapter 3
Overview of Machine Learning Approaches

ABSTRACT

This chapter enlists and presents an overview of various machine learning approaches. It also explains the machine learning techniques used in the area of software engineering domain especially case-based reasoning method. Case-based reasoning is used to predict software quality of the system by examining a software module and predicting whether it is faulty or non-faulty. In this chapter an attempt has been made to propose a model with the help of previous data which is used for prediction. In this chapter, how machine learning technique such as case-based reasoning has been used for error estimation or fault prediction. Apart from case-based reasoning, some other types of learning methods have been discussed in detail.

INTRODUCTION

This chapter presents an overview of machine learning approaches. It summarizes a variety of machine learning techniques in the domain of software engineering field (Zhang & Tsai, 2002).

Machine Learning (ML) is the study of computational methods to automate the process of knowledge acquisition from examples. ML algorithms have been utilized in several different problem domains. Some typical applications are: data mining problems where big databases contain important implicit regularities that can be revealed automatically; weakly understood domains

DOI: 10.4018/978-1-5225-3185-2.ch003

where there is a lack of knowledge needed to develop effective algorithms; or domains where programs must dynamically adapt to changing conditions (Mitchell, 1997). There are some list of publications and web sites offers a good starting point for the interested reader to be up to date with the state-of-the practice in ML applications (Aha, n.d.a, n.d.b; Bergadano & Gunetti, 1995; Bratko & Muggleton, 1995; Langley & Simon, 1995; Mendonca & Sunderhaft, 1999; Khoshgoftaar & Allen, 1999; Michalski, Bratko, & Kubat, 1998; Mitchell, 1997; Quinlan, 1990; Saitta & Neri, 1998; Sutton & Barto, 1999). To better use ML methods as tools to solve real world software engineering problems, we need to have a visible understanding of both the problems, and the tools and methodologies utilized. Since solutions to a given problem can frequently be expressed (or approximated) as a target function, the problem-solving process (or the learning process) boils down to how to find such a function that can best describe the known and unknown causes or phenomena for a given problem domain. Learning a target function (or a set of possible target functions) from training data involves the following issues:

- Representation

Dissimilar learning methods may accept dissimilar representation formalisms for the data and knowledge (functions) to be learned. In some learning method, the target function is not explicitly defined.

- Characteristics of the learning process

Learning can be supervised or unsupervised. Different methods may have a different inductive bias, different search approach, different guiding issue in the search, and different need regarding the availability of a domain theory.

For a target function, its generalization can be eager (at learning stage) or lazy (at classification stage), and its approximation can be obtained either locally or globally with regard to a set of training cases. Learning can result in either knowledge augmentation or knowledge (re) compilation. Depending on the interaction between a learner and its environment, there can be queried learning or reinforcement learning.

- Properties of training data and domain theories:

Data gathered in the learning process can be small or large in quantity, noisy or accurate in terms of arbitrary errors. Data can have different valuations.

Different learning methods can have different criteria regarding training data, with some methods requiring large amount of data, others being very sensitive to the quality of data, and yet another needing both training data and a domain theory. On the other hand, the quality of domain theories (completeness correctness) will have a direct impact on the result of analytical learning methods. Finally, based on the way in which the training data are generated and provided to the learner, there are batch learning and online learning.

- Target function output:

Depending on the output, learning problems can be categorized as twofold classification, multi-value classification and regression.

- Theoretical underpinnings and practical considerations:

Underpinning learning methods are different justifications: statistical, probabilistic, or logical. There are many different types of learning methods, each having its own characteristics and lending itself to certain learning problems.

Major types of learning methods may be classified (Mitchell, 1997) into the following groups: artificial neural networks (ANN), decision tree (DTL) learning, concept learning (CL), Bayesian learning (BL), reinforcement learning (RL), genetic algorithms (GA) and genetic programming (GP), instance-based learning (IBL, of which case-based reasoning, or CBR, is a popular method), inductive logic programming (ILP), analytical learning (AL, of which explanation-based learning, or EBL is a method), and combined inductive and analytical learning (IAL).There are algorithms for each of the above mentioned types of learning. The interested readers may refer to (Mitchell, 1997; Zhang & Tsai, 2002) for details.

WHAT IS MACHINE LEARNING?

Machine learning deals with the issue of how to build programs that improve their performance at some task through experience (Mitchell, 1997). Machine Learning is a scientific field addressing the question 'How can we program systems to automatically learn and to improve with experience?' I study learning from many kinds of experience, such as learning to predict which medical patients will respond to which treatments, by analyzing experience captured in databases of online medical records. I also study mobile robots that learn how to successfully navigate based on experience they gather from sensors as they roam their environment, and computer aids for scientific discovery that combine initial scientific hypotheses with new experimental data to automatically produce refined scientific hypotheses that better fit observed data. To tackle these problems, I develop algorithms that discover general conjectures and knowledge from specific data and experience, based on sound statistical and computational principles. I also develop theories of learning processes that characterize the fundamental nature of the computations and experience sufficient for successful learning in machines and in humans (Zhang & Tsai, 2002).

Machine learning has been utilized in various problem domains.

Some typical applications of machine learning are (Rashid, Patnayak, & Bhattacherjee, 2012):

- Optical character recognition
- Face detection
- Spam filtering
- Fraud detection
- Medical diagnosis
- Weather estimation

Major Categories of Machine Learning Techniques

Rule Induction (RI)

Rule induction is a field of machine learning where formal rules are extracted from a set of remarks (http://en.wikipedia.org/wiki/Rule_induction). Rule induction is one of the most significant techniques of machine learning and it is one of the basic tools of data mining at the same time. It is the method of reasoning by inferring generalizations based on individual instances. The Engineer Online (2006) "A pioneering study at Manchester University is using a 'robot scientist' to examine blood samples for biological markers that may diagnose Alzheimer's disease." The robot scientist combines the automatic operation of a blood analysis technique called GCGC-MS with artificial intelligence to determine which experiment to carry out next." Douglas Kell, a professor of Bioanalytical Science at Manchester, was one of the developers of the robot scientist. "The original idea was to automate the process of scientific discovery," said Kell. 'There is a model by which we alternate the world of ideas with the world of experience. We carry out an experiment then revise our hypobook in a cyclic loop. The robot scientist can combine working out what experiment is best to do next with actually carrying it out.' The robot uses Inductive Logic Programming, a machine learning process. The scientists give it the background knowledge about the experiment, called the domain. It then decides which hypobook to follow using the available data.

Neural Networks (NN)

Learning by Training a Network or Connectionist System. The human brain is an extremely impressive information processor, even though it "works" quite a bit slower than an ordinary computer. ANN is a gathering of such neurons interconnected in some precise manner. The organization of the brain has been taken many researchers as a model for building intelligent machines. One can think of a sort of "analogy" between the complex webs of interconnected neurons in a brain and the densely-interconnected units making up an artificial neural network (ANN), where each unit is massively interconnected just like a biological neuron. It is responsible for our ability to learn from examples. Even the death of some neuron does not create any problem, that's why it is robust. ANN is capable of taking in a number of inputs and producing an output. The human brain has about 10^{11} neurons, each connected, on average, to 10^4 others. Neuron activity is typically excited or inhibited through connections to other neurons. In comparison to computer the fastest neuron switching times is known to be 10^{-3} seconds, which is quite slow compared to computer switching speeds of 10^{-10} seconds. For instance, it requires about 10^{-1} seconds to visually recognize things (Mitchell, 1997).

Genetic Algorithms (GA)

Genetic algorithms are based on a biological symbol. It is search–based algorithm on the basis of natural genetics and natural selection. Genetic algorithm has been developed by John Holland and his colleagues for the goals of their research (Zhang & Tsai, 2002). The view is learning as a competition among a population of evolving candidate problem solutions. A robustness function evaluates each solution to decide whether it will supply to the subsequent generation of solutions. Then, through operations analogous to gene transfer in sexual imitation, the algorithm creates a new population of candidate solutions (Luger, 2002).

Inductive Logic Programming (ILP)

Inductive Logic Programming, a term introduced by Stephen Muggleton (1991). It is a subfield of machine learning; this uses logic programming as a consistent representation. Inductive Logic Programming (ILP) is a research area formed at the intersection of machine learning and logic programming. ILP systems develop predicate descriptions from examples and background knowledge. The examples, background knowledge and final descriptions are all described as logic programs. A unifying theory of ILP is being built up around lattice-based concepts such as refinement, least general generalization, inverse resolution and most specific corrections.

Inductive logic programming is mainly useful in bioinformatics and natural language processing. Presently successful application areas for ILP systems include the learning of structure-activity rules for drug design, finite-element mesh analysis design rules, primary-secondary prediction of protein structure and fault diagnosis rules for satellites.

Case-Based Reasoning (CBR)

Case-Based Reasoning (CBR) is one of the most popular machine learning technique first dignified in the year 1980s from the effort of Schank and others (Schank, 1982). CBR is a prosperous model for reasoning and learning in artificial intelligence, with major research efforts and growing applications extending the frontiers of the field. Case-based reasoning (CBR) is a problem-solving paradigm that is fundamentally different from other major AI approaches, in that instead of relying solely on general knowledge of a problem domain it uses specific cases (Abran & Robillard, 1996). Contrary to making an association along generalized relationships between problem descriptors and conclusion, CBR utilizes the specific knowledge of previously experienced, concrete problem situations (cases). Finding a similar past case, and reusing it in the new problem situation: this is the technique of CBR to solve a new problem. A second important difference is that CBR is also an approach to incremental, sustained learning where a new experience is retained each time a problem has been solved, making it available for future problems.

Thus, the notion of case-based reasoning does not only denote a particular reasoning method, irrespective of how the cases are acquired, it also denotes a machine learning paradigm that enables sustained learning by updating the case base after a problem has been solved. Learning in CBR takes place as a natural byproduct of problem solving. When a problem is successfully solved, the experience is retained in order to solve similar problems in the future. When an attempt to solve a problem fails, the reason for the failure is identified and remembered in order to avoid the same mistake in the future. Case-based reasoning prefers learning from experience, since it is usually easier to learn by retaining a concrete problem solving experience than to generalize from it.

- **Case-Based Problem Solving**

The basic idea of CBR is that 'similar problems have similar solutions' (Finnie & Sun, 2003). Reasoning by re-using past cases is a powerful and frequently applied method to solve problems for humans. For example, a physician treats a patient by recalling his past experience with a similar patient having similar symptoms. A manager handles a particular situation by recalling his past experience in a similar situation and a student solves certain numerical based on his past experience with similar problems. In all the above situations, a person recalls his past experience in a similar situation in which they may have been successful or unsuccessful. This common observation has also been supported by results from cognitive psychological research. Dominating role of specific, previously experienced situations in human problem solving has been confirmed in several studies conducted in this area. A theory of learning and reminding based on retaining of experience in a dynamic, evolving memory structure was developed by Schank (1982). Anderson demonstrated that people tend to use past cases as models, particularly in early learning. It has also been observed that even experts depend much on this technique of using past experiences for new problem. A case usually denotes a problem situation in CBR terminology. Hence, to solve a problem we use a previously experienced situation that has been captured and learned in a way that it can be reused in the solving of future problems. Hence, in CBR terminology, this experience is referred to as a past case, previous case, stored case, or retained case. Thus Case-based reasoning is—in effect—a cyclic and integrated process of solving a problem, learning from experience, solving a new problem, etc. It is to be noted that the term problem solving is used here in a wide sense, coherent with common practice within the area of knowledge-based systems in general. This means that problem solving does not deal with a concrete solution to an application problem, it may be just another problem put forth by the user. Hence problem solving situations may include justification or criticism of a solution proposed by the user, interpret a problem situation, generate a set of possible solutions, or generation of expectations in observable data.

• Learning in Case-Based Reasoning

A very important feature of case-based reasoning is its coupling to learning. The driving force behind case-based methods has to a large extent come from the machine learning community, and case-based reasoning is also regarded a subfield of machine learning (Aamodt, 1993). Thus, the notion of case-based reasoning does not only denote a particular reasoning method, irrespective of how the cases are acquired, it also denotes a machine learning paradigm that enables sustained learning by updating the case base after a problem has been solved. Learning in CBR occurs as a natural byproduct of problem solving. When a problem is successfully solved, the experience is retained in order to solve similar problems in the future. When an attempt to solve a problem fails, the reason for the failure is identified and remembered for obvious reason of not repeating that case-based reasoning finds it more appropriate to learn from experience, since it is usually easier to learn by retaining a concrete problem solving experience than to generalize from it. Still, effective learning in CBR requires a well worked out set of methods in order to extract relevant knowledge from the experience, integrate a case into an existing knowledge structure, and index the case for later matching with similar cases.

• Combining Cases with Other Knowledge

By examining theoretical and experimental results from cognitive psychology, it seems clear that human problem solving and learning in general is a process that involves the representation and utilization of several types of knowledge, and the combination of several reasoning methods. If cognitive plausibility is a guiding principle, architecture for intelligence where the reuse of cases is at the center, should also incorporate other and more general types of knowledge in one form or another. This is an issue of current concern in CBR research (Strube, 1991).

• Fundamentals of Case-Based Reasoning Methods

Central tasks that all case-based reasoning methods have to deal with are to identify the current problem situation, find a past case similar to the new one, use that case to suggest a solution to the current problem, evaluate the proposed solution, and update the system by learning from this experience. How this is done, what part of the process that is focused, what type of problems that drives the methods, etc. varies considerably, however, below is an attempt to classify CBR methods into types with roughly similar properties in this respect (Aamodt & Plaza, 1994).

Main Types of CBR Methods

The CBR paradigm covers a range of different methods for organizing, retrieving, utilizing and indexing the knowledge retained in past cases. Cases may be kept as concrete experiences, or a set of similar cases may form a generalized case. Cases may be stored as separate knowledge units, or split up into subunits and distributed within the knowledge structure. Cases may be indexed by a prefixed or open vocabulary, and within a flat or hierarchical index structure. The solution from a previous case may be directly applied to the present problem, or modified according to the differences between the two cases. The matching of cases, adaptation of solutions, and learning from an experience may be guided and supported by a deep model of general domain knowledge, by more shallow and compiled knowledge, or be based on an apparent, syntactic similarity only. CBR methods may be purely self-contained and automatic, or they may interact heavily with the user for support and guidance of its choices. Some CBR method assumes a rather large amount of widely distributed cases in its case base, while others are based on a more limited set of typical ones. Past cases may be retrieved and evaluated sequentially or in parallel. Actually, "case-based reasoning" is just one of a set of terms used to refer to systems of this kind. This has led to some confusions, particularly since case-based reasoning is a term used both as a generic term for several types of more specific approaches, as well as for one such approach. To some extent, this can also be said for analogical reasoning. An attempt of a classification, although not resolving the confusions, of the terms related to case-based reasoning is discussed below (Aamodt & Plaza, 1994).

- ## Exemplar-Based Reasoning

The term is derived from a classification of different views to concept definition into "the classical view", "the probabilistic view", and "the exemplar view". In the exemplar view, a concept is defined extensionally, as the set of its exemplars. CBR methods that address the learning of concept definitions (i.e., the problem addressed by most of the research in machine learning), are sometimes referred to as an exemplar-based. Examples are early papers by Kibler and Aha (1987), and Bareiss and Porter (1986). In this approach, solving a problem is a classification task, i.e., finding the right class for the unclassified exemplar. The class of the most similar past case becomes the solution to the classification problem. The set of classes constitutes the set of possible solutions. Modification of a solution found is therefore outside the scope of this method.

- ## Instance-Based Reasoning

This is a specialization of exemplar-based reasoning into a highly syntactic CBR-approach. To compensate for lack of guidance from general background knowledge, a relatively large number of instances are needed in order to close in on a concept definition. The representation of the instances is usually simple (e.g. Feature vectors), since a major focus is to study, automated learning with no user in the loop. Instance-based reasoning labels recent work by Kibler and Aha (1991), and serves to distinguish their methods from more knowledge-intensive exemplar-based approaches (e.g., Protos' methods). Basically, this is a non-generalized approach to the concept learning problem addressed by classical, inductive machine learning methods.

- ## Memory-Based Reasoning

This approach emphasizes a collection of cases as a large memory, and reasoning as a process of accessing and searching in this memory. Memory organization and access is a focus on the case-based methods. The utilization of parallel processing techniques is a characteristic of these methods, and distinguishes this approach from the others. The access and storage methods may rely on purely syntactic criteria, as in the MBR-Talk system (Stanfill & Waltz, 1988) or they may attempt to utilize general domain knowledge, as in PARADYME and the work done in Japan on massive parallel memories (Kitano, 1993).

- **Analogy-Based Reasoning**

This term is sometimes used, as a synonym to case-based reasoning, to describe the typical case-based approach (Khoshgoftaar & Seliya, 2003). However, it is also often used to characterize methods that solve new problems based on past cases from a different domain, while typical case-based methods focus on indexing and matching strategies for single-domain cases. Research on analogy reasoning is therefore a subfield concerned with mechanisms for identification and utilization of cross-domain analogies (Hall, 1989; Kedar-Cabelli, 1988). The major focus of study has been on the reuse of a past case, what is called the mapping problem: Finding a way to transfer, or map, the solution of an identified analogue (called source or base) to the present problem (called target).

ANALYSIS

Aamodt and Plaza (1994) broadly categorize the four primary steps comprising a CBR estimation system as:

1. Retrieve: the most similar case or cases
2. Reuse: the information and knowledge in that case to solve the problem
3. Revise: the proposed solution
4. Retain: the parts of this experience likely to be useful for future problem solving

A new problem is solved by retrieving one or more previously experienced cases, reusing the case in one way or another, revising the solution based on reusing a previous case, and retaining the new experience by incorporating it into the existing knowledge-base (case-base). An initial description of a problem defines a new case. This new case is used to RETRIEVE a case from the collection of previous cases. The retrieved case is combined with the new case - through REUSE - into a solved case, i.e. A proposed solution to the initial problem. Through the REVISE process this solution is tested for success, e.g. By being applied to the real-world environment or evaluated by a teacher, and repaired if failed. During RETAIN, useful experience is retained for future reuse, and the case base is updated by a new learned case, or by modification of some existing cases.

Figure 1. CBR schema

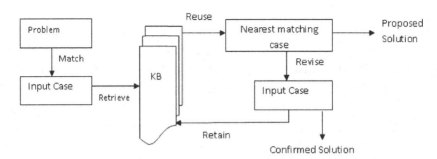

As indicated in the Figure 1 (Rashid, Patnayak, & Bhattacherjee, 2012), general knowledge (KB), usually plays a part in this cycle, by supporting the CBR processes. By general knowledge we here mean general domain-dependent knowledge, as opposed to specific knowledge embodied by the cases. For example, in diagnosing a patient by retrieving and reusing the case of a previous patient, a model of anatomy together with causal relationships between pathological states may constitute the "domain" knowledge used by a CBR system.

CONCLUSION

The case-based reasoning is dependent on data on similar projects. A case-based reasoning (CBR) system is an expert system that aims at finding solutions to a new problem based on previous experience, represented by cases in a knowledgebase. Each case is indexed for quick retrieval according to the problem domain. A solution process algorithm uses a similarity function to measure the relationship between the new problem and each case. The algorithm retrieves relevant cases and determines a solution to the new problem. The CBR approach may be applied to software quality estimation since CBR has several advantages over other software quality estimation modeling techniques.

- CBR method reflects the same method that human experts use when making estimates by applying analogical reasoning.
- CBR can handle both quantitative and qualitative data.
- CBR is simple and flexible, compared to algorithmic models.

- CBR can effectively support all the steps in the software quality estimation process for storing past cases, retrieving similar cases to adapting the retrieved case for the new project.
- The CBR approach takes advantage of expert prior knowledge.

REFERENCES

Aamodt, A. (1993). Explanation-driven retrieval, reuse, and learning of cases (SEKI Report SR-93-12). *Proceedings of the First European Workshop on Case-Based Reasoning EWCBR-93*, 279-284.

Aamodt, A., & Plaza, E. (1994). Case-Based Reasoning: Foundational Issues, Methodological Variations, and System Approaches. *AI Communications*, *7*(1), 39–59.

Abran, A., & Robillard, P. N. (1996). Function Points Analysis: An Empirical Study of its Measurement Processes. *IEEE Transactions on Software Engineering*, *22*(12), 895–909. doi:10.1109/32.553638

Aha, D. (n.d.a). *Case-based reasoning resources*. Retrieved from www.aic.nrl.navy.mil/~aha/research/case-basedreasoning.html

Aha, D. (n.d.b). *Machine learning resources*. Retrieved from www.aic.nrl.navy.mil/~aha/research/machinelearning.html

Aha, D., Kibler, D., & Albert, M. K. (1991). Instance-Based Learning Algorithms. *Machine Learning*, *6*(1).

Bergadano, F., & Gunetti, D. (1995). *Inductive Logic Programming: from Machine Learning to Software Engineering*. MIT Press.

Bratko, I., & Muggleton, S. (1995). Applications of inductive logic programming. *Communications of the ACM*, *38*(11), 65–70. doi:10.1145/219717.219771

Finnie, G. R., & Sun, Z. (2003). R5 model for case-based reasoning. *Knowledge-Based Systems*, *16*(1), 59–65. doi:10.1016/S0950-7051(02)00053-9

Hall, R. P. (1989). Computational approaches to analogical reasoning: A comparative analysis. *Artificial Intelligence*, *39*(1), 39–120. doi:10.1016/0004-3702(89)90003-9

Kedar-Cabelli, S. (1988). Analogy - from a unified perspective. In D. H. Helman (Ed.), Analogical reasoning (pp. 65-103). Kluwer Academic.

Khoshgoftaar, T. M., & Allen, E. B. (1999). Predicting fault-prone software modules in embedded systems with classification trees. *Proceedings of the 4th IEEE International Symposium on High-Assurance Systems Engineering.* IEEE. doi:10.1109/HASE.1999.809481

Khoshgoftaar, T. M., & Seliya, N. (2003). Analogy-based practical classification rules for software quality estimation. *Empirical Software Engineering Journal, 8*(4), 325–350. doi:10.1023/A:1025316301168

Kibler, D., & Aha, D. (1987). Learning representative exemplars of concepts; An initial study. *Proceedings of the Fourth International Workshop on Machine Learning,* 24-29. doi:10.1016/B978-0-934613-41-5.50006-4

Kitano, H. (1993). Challenges for massive parallelism. *Proceedings of the Thirteenth International Conference on Artificial Intelligence IJCAI-93,* 813-834.

Langley, P., & Simon, H. (1995). Applications of machine learning and rule induction. *Communications of the ACM, 38*(11), 55–64. doi:10.1145/219717.219768

Luger, G. F. (2002). Artificial Intelligence, Structures and Strategies for Complex Problem Solving (4th ed.). Harlow, UK: Addison-Wesley.

Mendonca, M., & Sunderhaft, N. L. (1999, September). *Mining software engineering data: a survey, DACS State-of-the-Art Report.* Retrieved from http://www.dacs.dtic.mil/techs/datamining/

Michalski, R. S., Bratko, I., & Kubat, M. (Eds.). (1998). *Machine Learning and Data Mining: Methods and Applications.* John Wiley & Sons Ltd.

Mitchell, T. (1997). Does machine learning really work? *AI Magazine, 18*(3), 11–20.

Mitchell, T. (1997). *Machine Learning.* McGraw-Hill.

Muggleton, S. (1991). Inductive logic programming. *New Generation Computing, 8*(4), 295–318. doi:10.1007/BF03037089

Porter, B., & Bareiss, R. (1986). PROTOS: An experiment in knowledge acquisition for heuristic classification tasks. *Proceedings of the First International Meeting on Advances in Learning (IMAL),* 159-174.

Quinlan, J. R. (1990). Learning logical definitions from relations. *Machine Learning, 5*(3), 239–266. doi:10.1007/BF00117105

Rashid, E., Patnayak, S., & Bhattacherjee, V. (2012). A Survey in the Area of Machine Learning and Its Application for Software Quality Prediction. *ACM SigSoft Software Engineering notes*, *37*(5). Retrieved from doi:10.1145/2347696.2347709

Saitta, L., & Neri, F. (1998). Learning in the real world. *Machine Learning*, *30*(2/3), 133–163. doi:10.1023/A:1007448122119

Schank, R. (1982). Dynamic Memory: A theory of reminding and learning in computers and people. Cambridge, UK: Cambridge University Press.

Stanfill, C., & Waltz, D. (1988). The memory based reasoning paradigm. In *Case based reasoning* (pp. 414–424). Clearwater Beach, FL: Morgan Kaufmann Publ.

Strube, G. (1991). The role of cognitive science in knowledge engineering. In F. Schmalhofer & G. Strube (Eds.), *Contemporary knowledge engineering and cognition: First joint workshop, proceedings* (pp. 161-174). Springer.

Sutton, R., & Barto, A. (1999). *Reinforcement Learning: An Introduction*. MIT Press.

Wikipedia. (2013, October 23). *Rule induction*. Retrieved October 23, 2013 from http://en.wikipedia.org/wiki/Rule_induction

Zhang, D., & Tsai, J. J. P. (2002). Advances in Machine Learning Applications in Software Engineering. Hershey, PA: Idea Group Publishing.

Zhang, D., & Tsai, J. J. P. (2002). *Machine learning and software engineering* (Technical Report TR-1). Department of Computer Science, California State University, Sacramento, CA.

Zhang, D., & Tsai, J. J. P. (2002). Machine Learning and Software Engineering. *Proceeding of the 14th IEEE International Conference on Tools with Artificial Intelligence (ICTAI)*.

Chapter 4

Methods of Software Quality Prediction With Similarity Measures:
As an Expert System

ABSTRACT

To improve the software quality the number of errors or faults must be removed from the software. This chapter presents a study towards machine learning and software quality prediction as an expert system. The purpose of this chapter is to apply the machine learning approaches such as case-based reasoning to predict software quality. Five different similarity measures, namely, Euclidean, Canberra, Exponential, Clark and Manhattan are used for retrieving the matching cases from the knowledgebase. The use of different similarity measures to find the best method significantly increases the estimation accuracy and reliability. Based on the research findings in this book it can be concluded that applying similarity measures in case-based reasoning may be a viable technique for software fault prediction

INTRODUCTION

The main aim of this chapter is to assess the case-based reasoning (CBR) as an expert system for software quality prediction with similarity measures (Rashid, Patnaik, & Bhattacherjee, 2014). Due to Lack of sufficient tools to

DOI: 10.4018/978-1-5225-3185-2.ch004

evaluate and predict software quality (fault) is one of the major challenges in software engineering field. Identifying and locating faults in software projects is a hard work. Particularly, when project sizes grow, this task becomes costly with complicated testing and evaluation mechanisms. On the other hand, measuring software in a continuous and disciplined manner brings many advantages such as accurate estimation of maintenance costs and schedules, and enhancing process and product qualities. Thorough study of software metric data also gives important clues about the position of possible faults in a module. The aim of this research is to establish a technique for identifying software faults using machine learning methods. It is very common to see large projects being undertaken nowadays. The software being developed in such projects goes through many phases of development and can be very complicated in terms of quality assessment. There will always be a concern for proper quality and effective cost estimation of such software. This can be rather tricky as the project being a large one may cover several unknown and unseen factors that might previously be very difficult to judge. Software fault prediction poses great challenges because fault data may not be available for the entire software module in the training data. In such cases machine learning technique like CBR can be successfully applied to fault diagnosis for customer service support. CBR systems use nearest neighbor algorithm for retrieval of cases from the Knowledgebase. Other machine learning techniques have also been extensively used for software quality (fault) prediction. The majority of today's software quality estimation models are built on using data from projects of a particular organization. Using such data has well known benefits such as ease of understanding and controlling of collecting data (Ganeasn, Khoshgoftaar, & Allen, 2002). But different researchers have reported contradictory results using different software quality estimation modeling techniques. It is still difficult to generalize many of the obtain results. This is due to the characteristics of the datasets being used and dataset's small size. Correct prediction of the software fault or maintain a software system is one of the most serious activities in managing software project. Software reliability provides measurement of software dependability in which probability of failure is generally time dependent. Various software quality characteristics have been suggested by authors such as James McCall and Barry Boehm. There have been differences in opinion regarding the exact definitions of the qualities of good software. For example maintainability has been used to define the ease with which an error can be located and rectified in the software. This definition also includes the ease with which changes can be incorporated in the software (Hughes & Cotterell, 1968).

BACKGROUND AND RELATED WORK

In the context of software fault prediction, most research works have focused on fault modules. The difficulty of software fault and maintainability is an important part of software project development. Software size and software fault data have regularly been used in the development of models that predict software quality. A few software quality models predict the quality of software modules as also faulty or non-faulty (Briand, Melo, & Wust, 2002; Khoshgoftaar & Seliya, 2003). Nowadays, one of the major application areas for case-based reasoning (CBR) in the field of health sciences, multiagent systems as well as in Web-based planning. The important issues of case-based reasoning were to reduce the maintenance cost, modifications of case base library or knowledgebase and these issues have been solved (Rashid, Patnaik, & Bhattacherjee, 2014). Research on CBR area is growing, but most of the systems are still prototypes and not available in the market as commercial products. However, many of the systems are intended to be commercialized (Begum et al., 2011). There is a little, but increasing piece of work in which machine learning method is used in the software quality (fault) prediction task. Recent age is more worried about the quality of software. Wide research is being carried out in this direction. The main thrust in modern software engineering research is centered on trying to build tools that can enhance software quality. Many researchers have used AI-Based approach like Case-Based Reasoning (CBR), Genetic Algorithm (GA), Neural Network (NN), etc. Khan et al. (2006) mentioned that, when software quality was predicted, the main objective was to predict reliability and stability of the software. Becker et al. (2006) predicted performance of the software. Zhong, Khoshgoftaar, and Selvia (2004) have used unsupervised Learning techniques to build a software quality estimation system. Case-based reasoning has also been used by Kadoda et al. (2000). Myrtveit and Stensrud (1999) and Ganesan, Khoshgoftaar, and Allen (2002) have also studied CBR was applied to software quality modeling of a family of complete industrial software systems and the accuracy is measured better than a corresponding multiple linear regression model in predicting the number of design faults. Aamodt and Plaza has given the case-based reasoning cycle. Richter and Weber (2013) have given that; case-based reasoning is a methodology for solving the new problems.

Rashid, Patnaik, and Bhattacherjee (2012, 2013) emphasized the importance of software quality prediction and accuracy of case-based estimation model.

LEARNING/PREDICTION SYSTEM

Machine learning techniques have the capability to predict software quality in the early stages of software development. Some of them can be applied if previous data (Training data) is available in the knowledgebase. In this research work we have used case-based reasoning (CBR) as a machine learning technique. The interactive learning / prediction system can be seen in figure 1. A user can access the prediction system using the given interface to learn new problems and get the predicted outputs (Rashid, Patnaik, & Bhattacherjee, 2014). The components of the prediction system are as follows:

1. Interface: It is the point of interaction.
2. Estimation/ Prediction system: Estimating or predicting a system is typically done by learning from the previous experience and provides knowledge for future solutions to some extent.
3. Machine learning algorithm: Case-based reasoning has been used as a machine learning algorithm where the method of solving a new case(s) based on the solutions on similar previous cases.

Figure 1. Interactive learning/prediction system

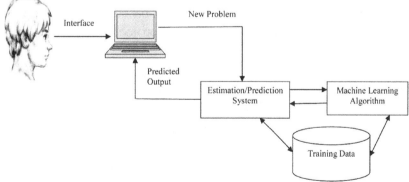

4. Training data: The training data used in this research work are collected from the B. Tech students of computer science and engineering from the college campus, written in high-level language (C and C++), They are maintained by faculty, supported by the laboratory staffs, resources like computers, software etc.

WHAT IS CASE-BASED REASONING (CBR)?

Case-Based Reasoning (CBR) is an important methodology for solving problems. It is one of the most popular machine learning technique first dignified in the year 1980s from the effort of Schank and others (Schank, 1982). The main purpose of CBR to solve the problems and these problems may be a variety of natures. But sometimes the formulation of the problem becomes difficult. Therefore, each and every problem formulation needs a different type of solution. For example:

What is the price of this bike? In this case, we have two answers for this

1. It could be too expensive for us.
2. Second answer could be 5 laks or more.

It is very important that one has to know the context where the problem is stated in order to get which answer is appropriate.

Fundamentally case-based reasoning consists of three words and needs to explain briefly (Weber & Richter, 2007):

1. Case: It is mainly an experience of a solved problem.
2. Based: Based means that the reasoning is based on experiences.
3. Reasoning: It means that the approach is projected to draw conclusions using experiences.

Models of CBR

I can broadly categorize the following five primary steps comprising a CBR estimation system (Rashid, Patnaik, & Bhattacherjee, 2014):

The following steps required when CBR applied, that is,

1. **Problem Formulation:** It needs to get the new problem from a user.
2. **Retrieve:** It retrieves similar or nearest case (s) from the KBS.

Figure 2. Different tasks in case-based reasoning process

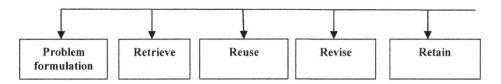

Figure 3. Context-level diagram

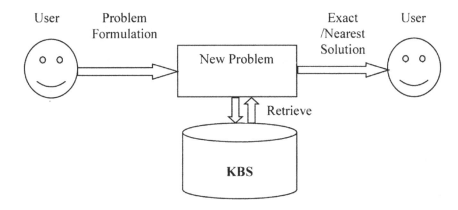

Figure 4. Reuse principle

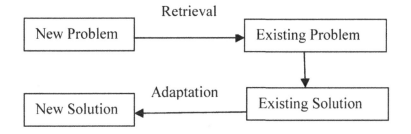

Figure 5. Conceptual CBR procedure

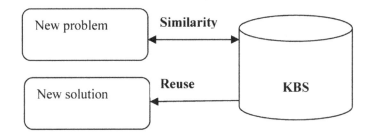

3.   **Reuse:** Reuse same solution for same problem.
4.   **Revise:** Modify the solution for new problem.
5.   **Retain:** Retain modified solution for future use.

See Figures 2, 3, 4, and 5, respectively (Rashid, Patnaik, & Bhattacherjee, 2014).

Case-based estimation comes in handy when limited domain knowledge is available and the optimum solution is difficult to be defined. An advantage of case-based estimation is that it is easy to comprehend and explain its process to practitioners. In addition, it can model a complex set of relationships between the dependent variables and the independent variables. The best working example of case-based reasoning is the complex human intelligence. However, our (human) reasoning by analogy is always more than approximate or vaguer rather than precise and certain.

SIMILARITY AND RETRIEVAL

Many literatures are reviewed on case-based reasoning and neural network (Thwin & Quah, 2002; Grosser, Sahraoui, & Valtchev, 2003; Liao, Zhang, & Mount, 1998). Similarity has been used for retrieval purposes. The difference between the input case and the retrieved case can be found out about the concept of the Euclidian distance, Manhattan distance, Clark distance, Canberra distance and Exponential distance. These measures are used to calculate the distance of the new record set or case from each record set stored in the knowledgebase. The matching case (s) is those that have the minimum distance from the new record set (Challagulla, Bastani, & Yen, 2006). The purposes of similarity functions are to retrieve the case (s) from the knowledgebase, which is most similar to a given new problem that their solutions can be swapped. Suppose a record set S1 of n fields has following values u1, u2, ..., un for the n fields respectively. Similarly, a record set S2 of the same type with field values v1, v2, ..., vn. Table 1 shows the definitions of five distance functions which is used in our analysis (Challagulla, Bastani, & Yen, 2006).

Table 1. Distance functions

Distance Dist (S1, S2) With Equal Weights of All Attributes
1) Euclidean distance ($dist_e$)
$$dist_e(S1, S2) = \sqrt{\sum_{i=1}^{n}(w_i(u_i - v_i))^2} \quad (1)$$
2) Manhattan distance ($dist_m$)
$$dist_m(S1, S2) = \sum_{i=1}^{n} w_i \mid u_i - v_i \mid \quad (2)$$
3) Canberra distance ($dist_c$)
$$dist_c(S1, S2) = \sum_{i=1}^{n} w_i \mid u_i - v_i \mid / \mid u_i + v_i \mid \quad (3)$$
4) Clark distance ($dist_{cl}$)
$$dist_{cl}(S1, S2) = \sum_{i=1}^{n} w_i \mid u_i - v_i \mid^2 / \mid u_i + v_i \mid^2 \quad (4)$$
5) Exponential distance ($dist_{ex}$)
$$dist_{ex}(S1, S2) = \sum_{i=1}^{n} w_i(e^d)$$ Where $d = \sqrt{(u_i - v_i)^2}$ (5)

METHODOLOGY

I observe software quality (fault) as a multi-dimensional idea, consisting of such properties of the software as maintainability, correctness, flexibility, error proneness, changeability, etc.

The metrics to be selected depends on the programming languages. The training data used in this chapter are collected from the B. Tech students of computer science and engineering from the college campus, written in high-level language (C and C++). Students are guided by their faculty, lab assistant, and resources like computers, software etc.

The following metrics include (Rashid, Patnaik, & Bhattacherjee, 2014):

- Size metrics (LOC)
- Code documentation metrics (comment lines, blank lines).
- Number of functions or procedures.
- Difficulty level of Software.
- Experience of Programmer in Year.
- Development Time.
- Number of variables.
- Number of functions or procedures + Lines of code (Combining more than one existing metric can also create new metric).

PROPOSED MODEL

The fundamental question in this model is how to set the feature weights, w_i, since the individual features should influence project similarity to a different degree (Auer et al., 2006). Various approaches have been proposed:

- Set all projects feature weights to identical values: $w_i = 1$, $i = 1 \dots n$.
- Set each project feature weights to a value determined by human judgment.
- Set each project feature weights to a value obtained by statistical analysis.
- Set each project feature weight either to 0 or 1 so that an estimation quality metric is maximized. This brute-force approach proposed by Shepperd and Schofield tries to identify a subset of important features. Once these features are identified, they are all given the same weight.

The parameters selected for the model were based upon the following assumptions (Rashid, Patnaik, & Bhattacherjee, 2014).

- The time constraint or development time affects the quality level.
- The mental discrimination required to design and code a program depends upon the numbers of functions and number of variable.
- The number of functions is a predictor of how much effort is required to develop a program.

- The programming language exposure / experience of a programmer affects the quality level.
- The inherent program difficulty level also affects the quality level.

Estimation Criteria

The fundamental requirement of evaluating and validating the methodology for the accuracy of estimations, we have used error prediction method i.e. Mean Magnitude of Relative Error (MMRE) to measure how accurate the estimations are. Relative error is the absolute error in the observations divided by its actual parameter. Improvements in accuracy of predictions and increasing the reliability of the knowledgebase were a priority. The research work present the results obtained when applying the case-based reasoning model to the data set. The accuracy of estimates is evaluated by using the magnitude of relative error (MRE) defined as (Rashid, Patnaik, & Bhattacherjee, 2014):

$$MRE = \left| \frac{Actual\_Parameter - Targeted\_Parameter}{Actual\_Parameter} \right| \tag{6}$$

Research Category

Figure 6. Components of an expert system

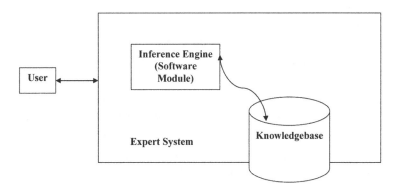

Case-based reasoning (CBR) is most popular machine learning technique. A CBR system is an expert system that aims at finding solutions to a new problem based on previous experience. Therefore, we can classify this research work as an "expert system" because system consists of a knowledgebase and a software module called the inference engine to perform inferences from the knowledgebase. These inferences are communicated to the user. Figure 6 shows the components of an expert system (Waterman, 2008).

Evaluating Error Predictions

The user requires a system that can search and find the exact/near matching case from the knowledgebase (KBS) using various distance functions. The novel idea behind this system is that KBS building is an important task in CBR and the KBS can be built based on world new problems along with world new solutions. In this research work; first, I have built a KBS. Second, I have given the emphasis on how to reduce the maintenance cost. For reducing the maintenance cost. I am removing the duplicate record set from the KBS. Third, the magnitude of relative error is calculated with the help of distance functions. In this research, I have used five distance function, namely Euclidean distance, Manhattan distance, Canberra distance, Clark distance and Exponential distance. As I continue making the model, I can identify the distance functions which are more efficient for error prediction. It seems that the model is application-based and it is very easy to extend this model to a theoretical case-based reasoning (CBR). As, I know that CBR cannot develop robustly without theoretical support. Following modules have been used which has given below (see Figure 7) (Rashid, Patnaik, & Bhattacherjee, 2014).

1. Accept Data Module: By this module new records are inserted manually in the knowledgebase. It takes the new record sets as input from the user. Each record set is assigned a unique Record ID by this module.
2. Save Module: It saves the new records into the knowledgebase.
3. Edit and Save Module: It accepts the Record ID of the record to be edited. Searches for the record set with the specified ID and allows the user to edit the record. After editing the record is saved.
4. Input Data Module: This module accepts the values of various parameters from the user. It also has the provision of assigning weights to the parameters if the user wants to do so.

Figure 7. Search-based error prediction systems with five similarity functions

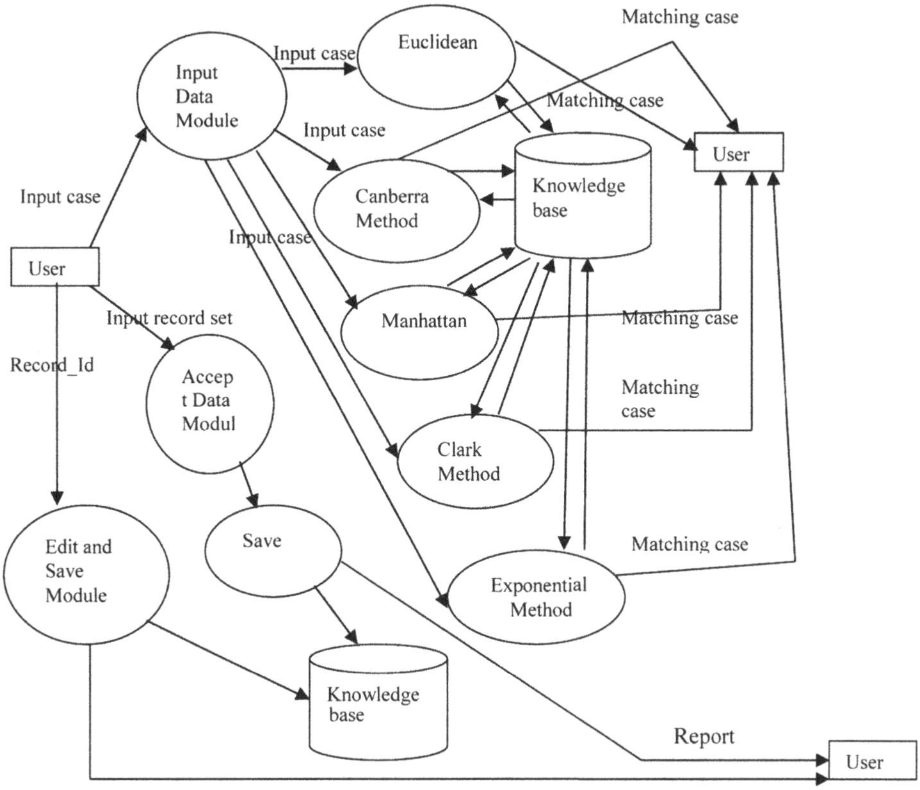

ADVANTAGES OF THIS RESEARCH

The biggest advantage of this research has been given below (Rashid, Patnaik, & Bhattacherjee, 2014):

1. A Knowledgebase (KBS) is created and maintained to store the cases as different parameters of the software against which the matching process has to be performed.
2. The objective is to predict the quality of the software project accurately and use the results in future predictions.
3. The matching has been done using various similarity measures like Euclidean, Manhattan, Canberra, Exponential and Clark.

45

4. The prediction is based upon Case-Based Reasoning (CBR) technique. CBR takes minimum time in comparison to other AI approach like Neural Network (NN) and Genetic Algorithm (GA). But for accuracy the data requirement for CBR, NN, GA are high (www.google.co.in/search?newwindow).

5. New features and functionalities can be added easily to the existing system to satisfy the future requirements (for example easy to extend).

6. The advantages of this research work are result-oriented because CBR systems use nearest neighbor algorithm for retrieval of cases from the Knowledgebase.

7. With the help of this technique we can improve the quality of the software through early prediction of error patterns.

8. Removing the duplicate record set from the KBS for reducing the maintenance cost. This technique can be successfully applied to fault diagnosis for client service support.

9. CBR technique can use existing solution and adapt it to the current situation.

10. To add new record set to CBR system, a user only needs to add new cases to the system.

11. The indigenous tool uses 'C' as the programming language.

Figure 8. Building of KBS

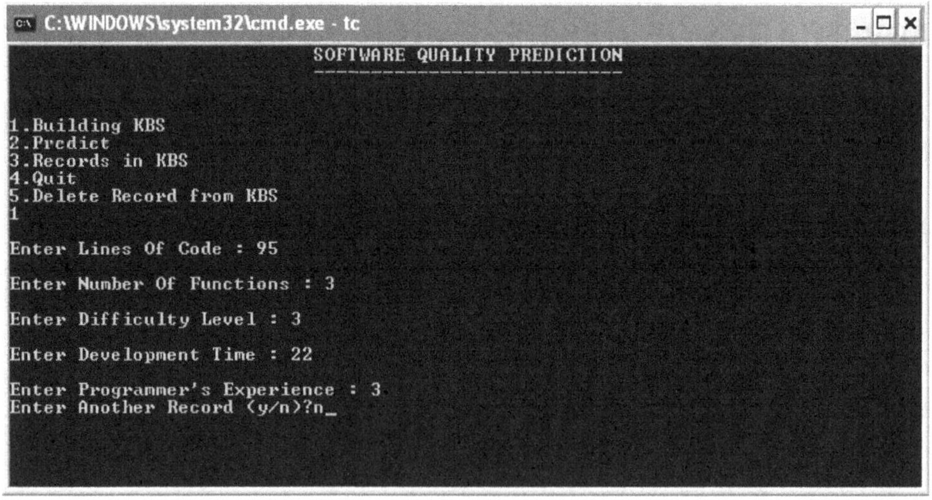

12. The indigenous tool can be readily deployed on any low configuration system and it would not impact its performance, as it does not rely on external runtimes and DLL's like the .NET programs rely on. The software is a console based application and thus does not use the GUI functions of the operating System, which makes it very fast in execution.

Figure 9. Software quality prediction technique

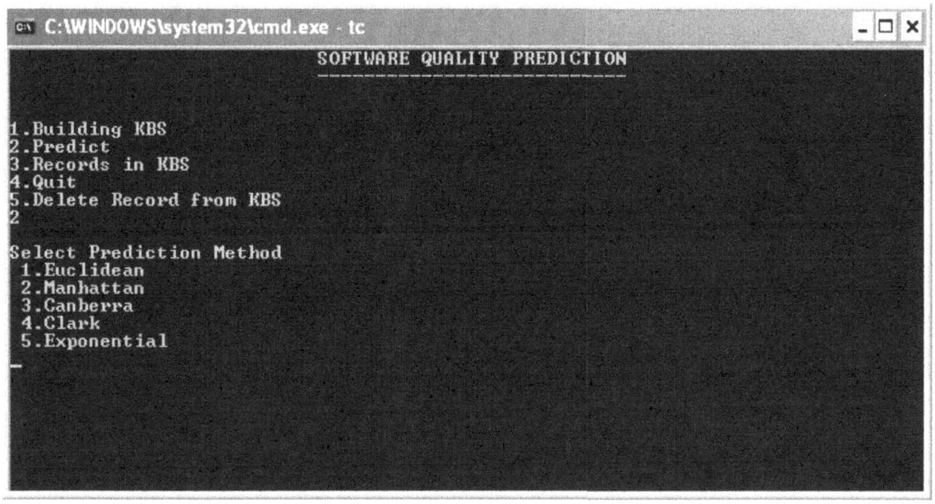

Figure 10. Selection of prediction method (Euclidean method)

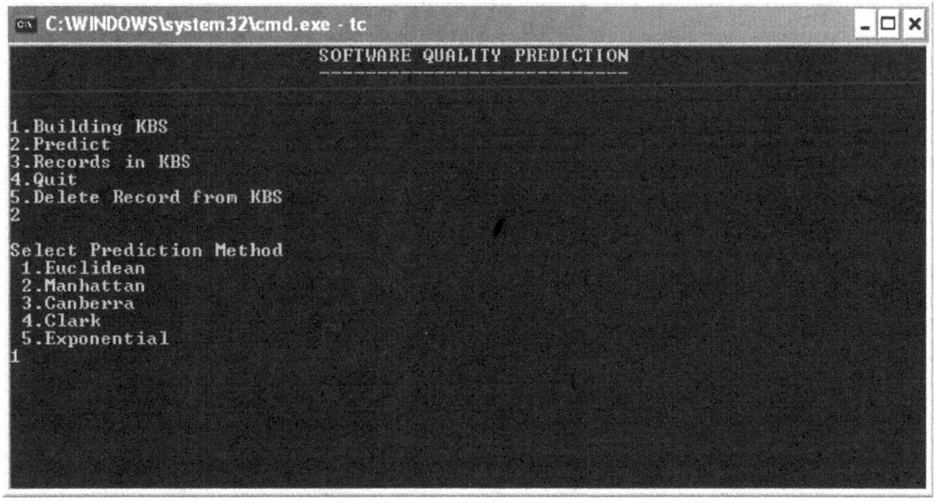

ANALYSIS AND RESULTS

The main objective of this prediction system is to help development of good quality software. The aim of the chapter is also to explore how case-based reasoning technique can support decision-making and help control dissimilarity in software fault activities, thus ultimately enhancing software quality.

Figure 11. Accuracy using Euclidean method

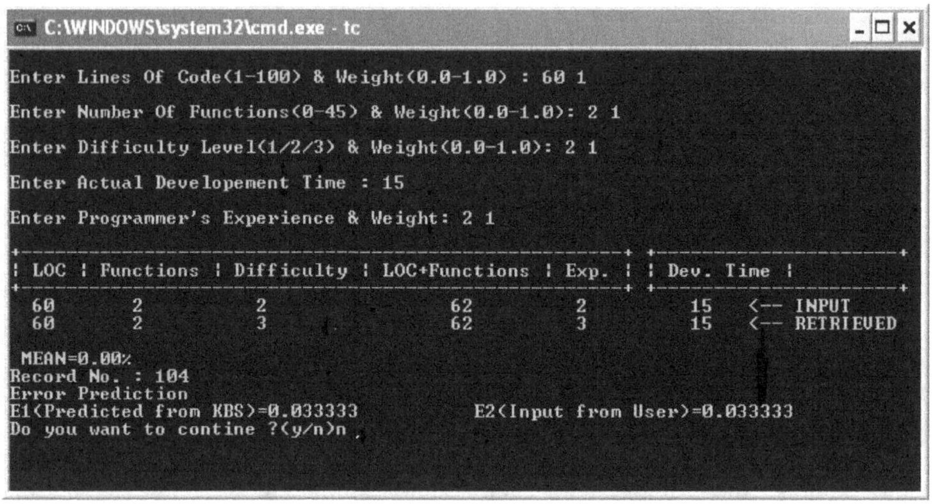

Figure 12. Selection of prediction method (Manhattan method)

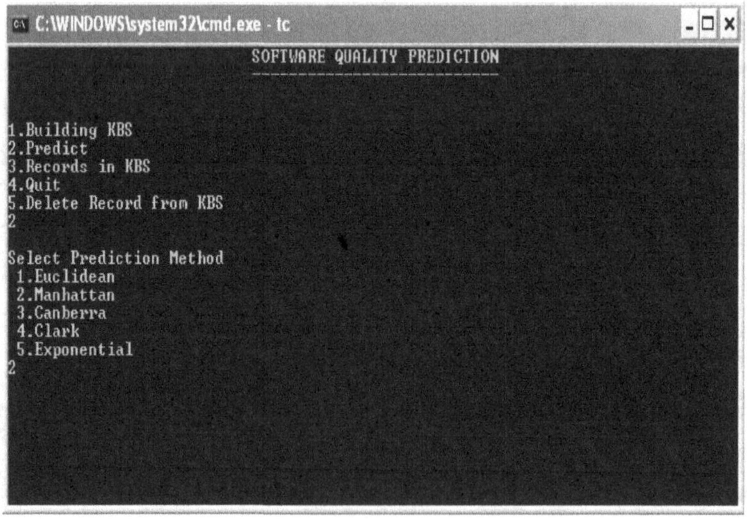

Estimating reliability of upcoming software versions based on fault history the fault estimation to enhance test stage effectiveness; task of resources to fix faults, and distinguishing faulty software modules from non-faulty ones. In this chapter, five distance functions used, i.e., Euclidean method, Canberra

Figure 13. Accuracy using Manhattan method

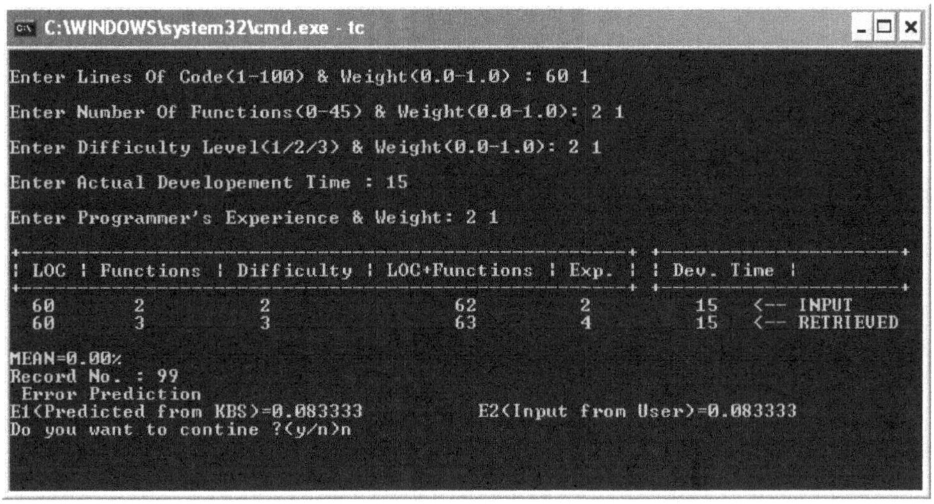

Figure 14. Selection of prediction method (Canberra method)

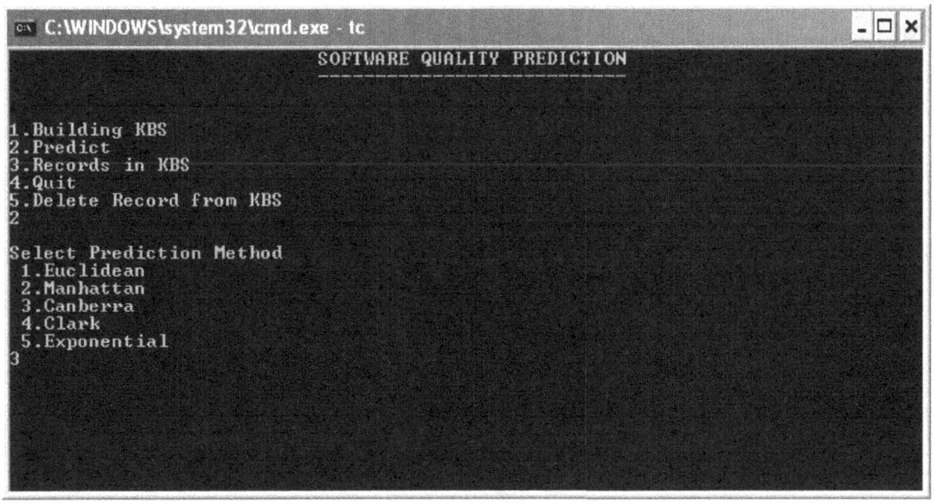

49

method, Clark method, Exponential method and Manhattan method, using these five distance functions how machine learning technique like case-based reasoning helps to predict exact matching case from the knowledge base. In this research, mean magnitude of relative error is calculated with the help of

Figure 15. Accuracy using Canberra method

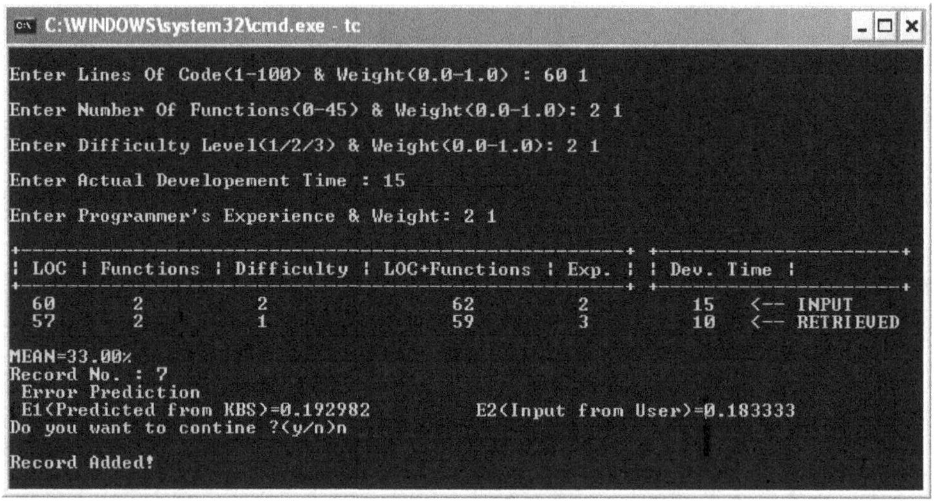

Figure 16. Selection of prediction method (Clark method)

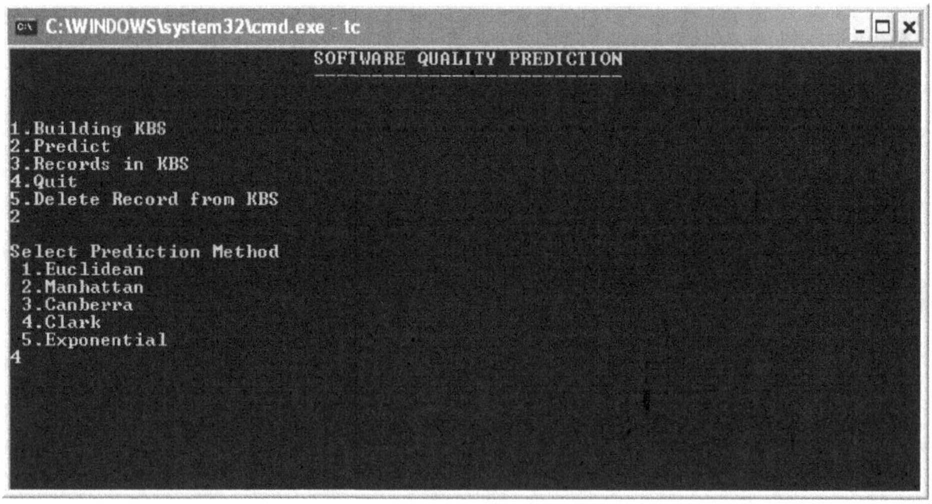

dependent variable i.e., development time. It was observed that when I was using the five distance function for the same data set, the results are coming quite good when I was using exponential distance. And a result is derived where acceptable range is within 10%. Figure 11, 13, 15, 17, and 19 shows the accuracy comparisons of different distance functions. As the number of exact matching case increases, the accuracy also increases. Therefore, I can

Figure 17. Accuracy using Clark method

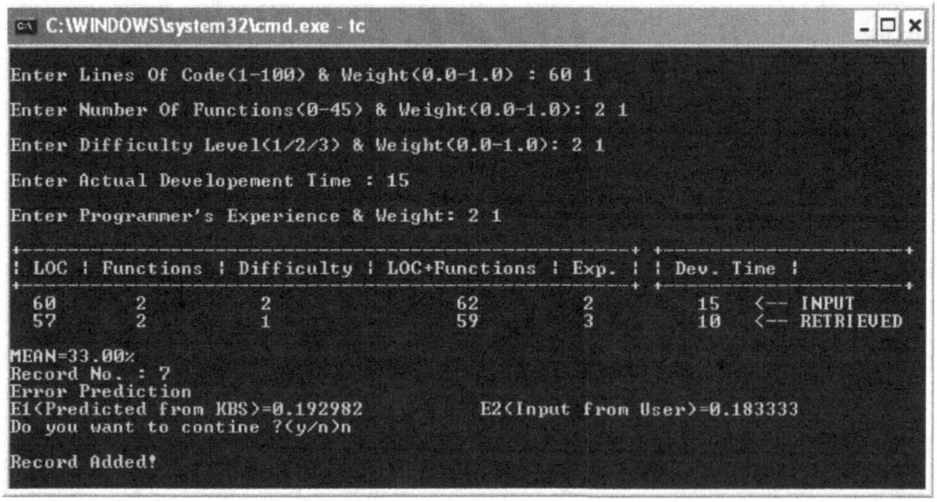

```
C:\WINDOWS\system32\cmd.exe - tc                                    _ □ ×

Enter Lines Of Code(1-100) & Weight(0.0-1.0) : 60 1

Enter Number Of Functions(0-45) & Weight(0.0-1.0): 2 1

Enter Difficulty Level(1/2/3) & Weight(0.0-1.0): 2 1

Enter Actual Developement Time : 15

Enter Programmer's Experience & Weight: 2 1

+-----------------------------------------------------------+ +------------------+
! LOC ! Functions ! Difficulty ! LOC+Functions ! Exp. ! ! Dev. Time !
+-----------------------------------------------------------+ +------------------+
   60       2            2              62          2          15   <-- INPUT
   57       2            1              59          3          10   <-- RETRIEVED
MEAN=33.00%
Record No. : 7
Error Prediction
E1(Predicted from KBS)=0.192982        E2(Input from User)=0.183333
Do you want to contine ?(y/n)n

Record Added!
```

Figure 18. Selection of prediction method (exponential method)

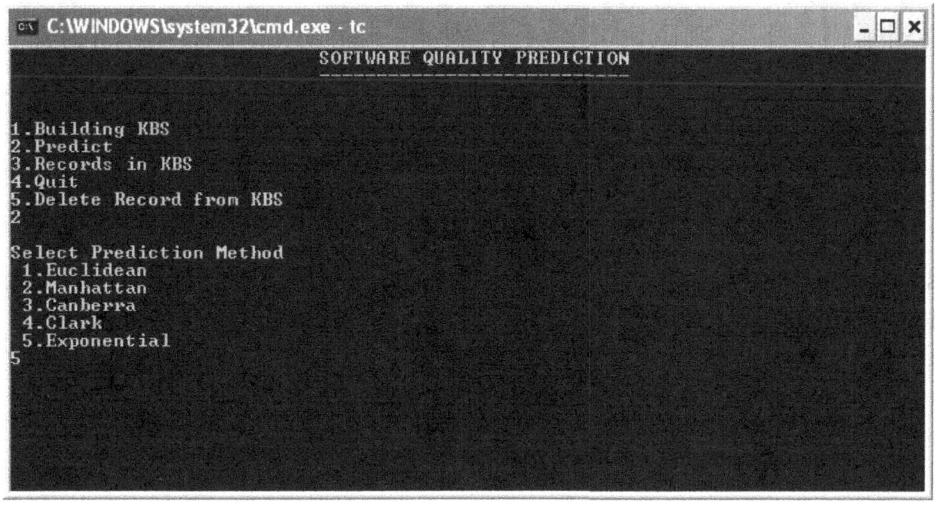

```
C:\WINDOWS\system32\cmd.exe - tc                                    _ □ ×
                        SOFTWARE QUALITY PREDICTION


1.Building KBS
2.Predict
3.Records in KBS
4.Quit
5.Delete Record from KBS
2

Select Prediction Method
 1.Euclidean
 2.Manhattan
 3.Canberra
 4.Clark
 5.Exponential
5
```

Figure 19. Accuracy using exponential method

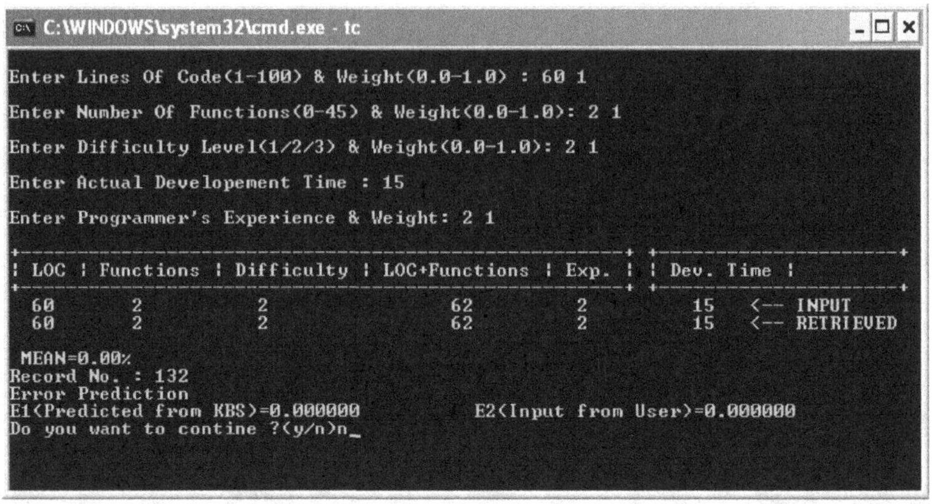

```
C:\WINDOWS\system32\cmd.exe - tc                                    _ □ ×

Enter Lines Of Code(1-100) & Weight(0.0-1.0) : 60 1

Enter Number Of Functions(0-45) & Weight(0.0-1.0): 2 1

Enter Difficulty Level(1/2/3) & Weight(0.0-1.0): 2 1

Enter Actual Developement Time : 15

Enter Programmer's Experience & Weight: 2 1
+----------------------------------------------------------+ +---------------------+
: LOC : Functions : Difficulty : LOC+Functions : Exp. : : Dev. Time :
+----------------------------------------------------------+ +---------------------+
  60        2            2              62          2           15    <-- INPUT
  60        2            2              62          2           15    <-- RETRIEVED

  MEAN=0.00%
Record No. : 132
Error Prediction
E1(Predicted from KBS)=0.000000          E2(Input from User)=0.000000
Do you want to contine ?(y/n)n_
```

Figure 20. Before deletion of duplicate record set the status of KBS

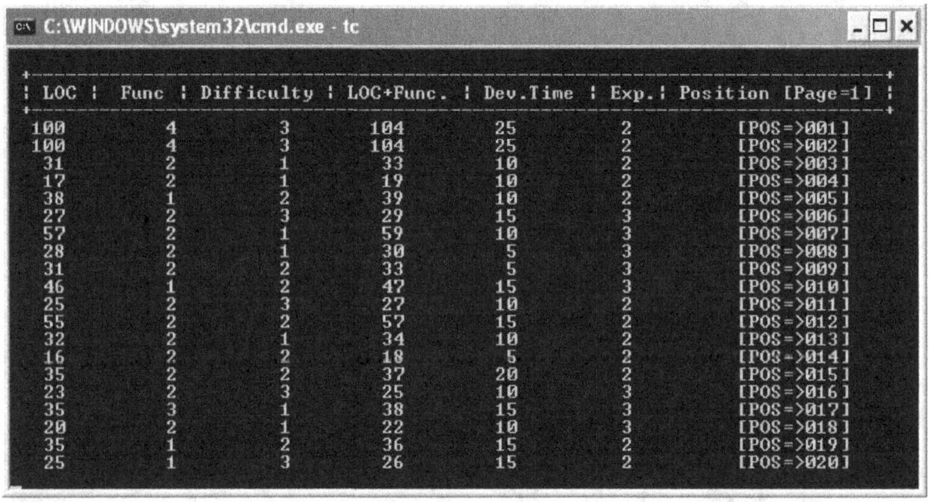

```
C:\WINDOWS\system32\cmd.exe - tc                                    _ □ ×

+------------------------------------------------------------------------------------+
: LOC :  Func : Difficulty : LOC+Func. : Dev.Time : Exp.: Position [Page=1] :
+------------------------------------------------------------------------------------+
  100     4        3          104         25         2      [POS=>001]
  100     4        3          104         25         2      [POS=>002]
   31     2        1           33         10         2      [POS=>003]
   17     2        1           19         10         2      [POS=>004]
   38     1        2           39         10         2      [POS=>005]
   27     2        3           29         15         3      [POS=>006]
   57     2        1           59         10         3      [POS=>007]
   28     2        1           30          5         3      [POS=>008]
   31     2        2           33          5         3      [POS=>009]
   46     1        2           47         15         3      [POS=>010]
   25     2        3           27         10         2      [POS=>011]
   55     2        2           57         15         2      [POS=>012]
   32     2        1           34         10         2      [POS=>013]
   16     2        2           18          5         2      [POS=>014]
   35     2        2           37         20         2      [POS=>015]
   23     2        3           25         10         3      [POS=>016]
   35     3        1           38         15         3      [POS=>017]
   20     2        1           22         10         3      [POS=>018]
   35     1        2           36         15         2      [POS=>019]
   25     1        3           26         15         2      [POS=>020]
```

say that exponential method is best for error prediction while using CBR technique. In this work, I display the error relative to the size metric retrieved from the knowledgebase (E1) and size metric of the user (E2). It can be seen in the form of figure (s) (See Figure 5 through Figure 19). Figures 20-22 shows the display before, during and after the Duplicate Data Set has been removed from KBS.

Figure 21. Duplicate record set deleted from KBS

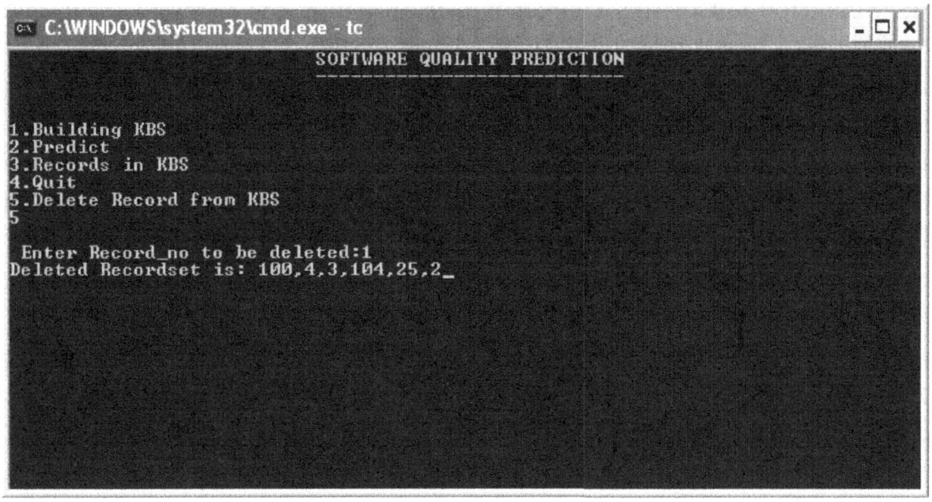

```
C:\WINDOWS\system32\cmd.exe - tc                                    _ □ ×
                        SOFTWARE QUALITY PREDICTION
                        ---------------------------

1.Building KBS
2.Predict
3.Records in KBS
4.Quit
5.Delete Record from KBS
5

 Enter Record_no to be deleted:1
Deleted Recordset is: 100,4,3,104,25,2_
```

Figure 22. After deletion of duplicate record set from KBS

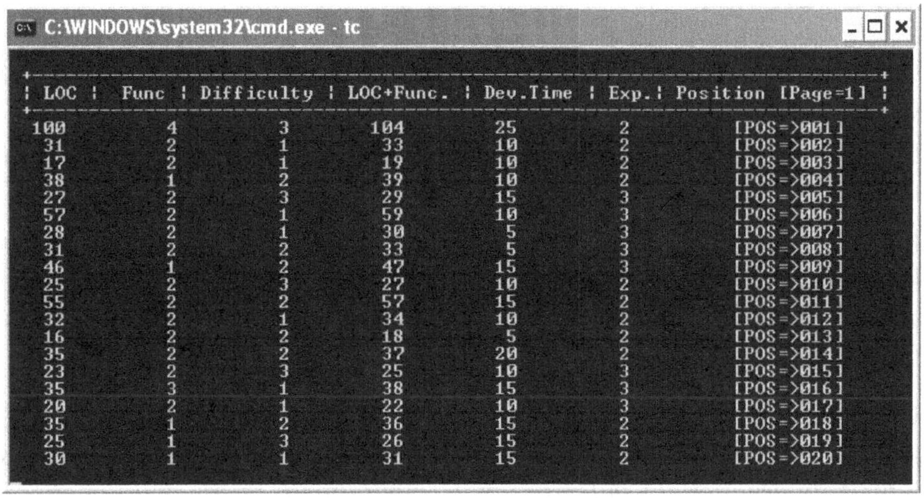

```
C:\WINDOWS\system32\cmd.exe - tc                                    _ □ ×
+-------+------+-----------+---------+----------+------+---------------------+
: LOC : Func : Difficulty : LOC+Func. : Dev.Time : Exp.: Position [Page=1] :
+-------+------+-----------+---------+----------+------+---------------------+
100      4       3           104        25         2      [POS=>001]
31       2       1           33         10         2      [POS=>002]
17       2       1           19         10         2      [POS=>003]
38       1       2           39         10         2      [POS=>004]
27       2       3           29         15         3      [POS=>005]
57       2       1           59         10         3      [POS=>006]
28       2       1           30         5          3      [POS=>007]
31       2       2           33         5          3      [POS=>008]
46       1       2           47         15         3      [POS=>009]
25       2       3           27         10         2      [POS=>010]
55       2       2           57         15         2      [POS=>011]
32       2       1           34         10         2      [POS=>012]
16       2       2           18         5          2      [POS=>013]
35       2       2           37         20         2      [POS=>014]
23       2       3           25         10         3      [POS=>015]
35       3       1           38         15         3      [POS=>016]
20       2       1           22         10         3      [POS=>017]
35       1       2           36         15         2      [POS=>018]
25       1       3           26         15         2      [POS=>019]
30       1       1           31         15         2      [POS=>020]
```

CONCLUSION

Reasoning by re-using past cases is a powerful and frequently applied way to solve problems for humans. For example, a physician treats a patient by recalling his past experience with a similar patient having similar symptoms. Similarly, in this research work, I have taken different attributes of the software as an input case and finding the best solution from the KBS. The main contribution of this chapter is a use of machine learning technique such as case-based reasoning as an expert system for predicting the fault in a software module with the help of distance functions. In this research work five distance functions the Euclidean, Canberra, Exponential, Clark and Manhattan method were taken into consideration in terms of percentage of errors generated during execution of programs. For their efficacy in determining errors, the low error programs detected by these methods may help to design error free programs. If the error estimation is less than 10%, then the input record set is auto saved to the knowledgebase. Once the result is predicted it is added to the database to enhance the accuracy of future predictions. Only those results are added that gives an error of 10% or less. But if the error estimation is more than 10%, then the input record set must be revised then save to the knowledgebase for future solutions. These data can be safely classified as high quality data.

REFERENCES

Rashid, E., Patnaik, S., & Bhattacherjee, V. (2014), Search-Based Information Retrieval and Fault prediction with distance functions. *International Journal of Software Engineering and its Applications*, 8(2), 75-86. doi:10.14257/ijseia.8.2.08

Rashid, E., Patnaik, S., & Bhattacherjee, V. (2014), Machine Learning and Software Quality Prediction: As an Expert System. *International Journal of Information Engineering and Electronic Business*, 6(2), 9-27. doi:.02.0210.5815/ijieeb

Rashid, E., Patnaik, S., & Bhattacherjee, V. (2014). Machine Learning and its application in Software fault prediction with similarity measures. *Proceedings of the 5th International Conference on Computational Vision and Robotic*.

Ganeasn, K., Khoshgoftaar, T. M., & Allen, E. (2002). Case-based Software Quality Prediction. *International Journal of Software Engineering and Knowledge Engineering*, 10(2), 139–152. doi:10.1142/S0218194000000092

Hughes, B., & Cotterell, M. (1968). *Software Project Management*. Tata McGraw-Hill.

Briand, L. C., Melo, W. L., & Wust, J. (2002). Assessing the applicability of fault-proneness models across object-oriented software projects. *IEEE Transactions on Software Engineering, 28*(7), 706–720. doi:10.1109/TSE.2002.1019484

Khoshgoftaar, T. M., & Seliya, N. (2003). Analogy-based practical classification rules for software quality estimation. *Empirical Software Engineering Journal, 8*(4), 325–350. doi:10.1023/A:1025316301168

Begum, S., Ahmed, M. U., Funk, P., Xiong, N., & Folke, M. (2011). Case-Based Reasoning Systems in the Health Sciences: A Survey of Recent Trends and Developments. *IEEE Transactions on Systems, Man, and Cybernetics, Part C: Applications and Reviews, 41*(4), 421-434. doi:10.1109/TSMCC.2010.2071862

Khan, M. J., Shamail, S., Awais, M. M., & Hussain, T. (2006) Comparative study of various artificial intelligence techniques to predict software quality. *Proceedings of the 10th IEEE multitopic conference INMIC*, 173-177. doi:10.1109/INMIC.2006.358157

Becker, S., Grunske, L., Mirandola, R., & Overhage, S. (2006), Performance prediction of component-based systems a survey from an engineering perspective. In Architecture systems with Trust-worthy components, LNCS (Vol. 3938). Springer.

Zhong, S., Khoshgoftaar, T. M., & Selvia, N. (2004) Unsupervised Learning for Expert-Based Software Quality Estimation. *Proceeding of the Eighth IEEE International Symposium on High Assurance Systems Engineering (HASE)*.

Kadoda, G., Cartwright, M., Chen, L., & Shepperd, M. (2000). Experiences Using Case-Based Reasoning to Predict Software Project Effort. *Proceeding of EASE*, 23-28.

Myrtveit, I., & Stensrud, E. (1999). A Controlled Experiment to Assess the Benefits of Estimating with Analogy and Regression Models. *IEEE Transactions on Software Engineering, 25*(4), 510–525. doi:10.1109/32.799947

Richter, M. M., & Weber, R. (2013). Case-Based Reasoning. Springer Verlag.

Rashid, E., Patnaik, S., & Bhattacherjee, V. (2013). Enhancing the accuracy of case-based estimation model through Early Prediction of Error Patterns. *Proceedings of the International Symposium on Computational and Business Intelligence*. doi:10.1109/ISCBI

Rashid, E., Patnaik, S., & Bhattacherjee, V. (2012). Software Quality Estimation Using Machine Learning: Case-Based Reasoning Technique. *International Journal of Computers and Applications*, *58*(14).

Weber, R. O., & Richter, M. M. (2007). *Case-Based Reasoning Research and Development*. Springer. Retrieved July 2014 from http://www.springer.com/computer/ai/book/978-3-540-74138-1

Thwin, M. M. T., & Quah, T.-S. (2002). Application of neural network for predicting software development faults using object-oriented design metrics. *Proceedings of the 9th International Conference on Neural Information Processing ICONIP'02*, 5. doi:10.1109/ICONIP.2002.1201906

Grosser, D., Sahraoui, H. A., & Valtchev, P. (2003). Analogy-based software quality prediction. *Proceedings of the 7th Workshop on Quantitative Approaches in Object-Oriented Software Engineering QAOOSE*.

Liao, T. W., Zhang, Z., & Mount, C. R. (1998). Similarity measures for retrieval in case-based reasoning systems. *Applied Artificial Intelligence*, *12*(4), 267–288.

Challagulla, V. U., Bastani, F. B., & Yen, I. L. (2006). A Unified Framework for Defect data analysis using the MBR technique. *Proceeding of the 18th IEEE International Conference on Tools with Artificial Intelligence (ICTAI)*.

Auer, M., Trendowicz, A., Graser, B., Haunschmid, E., & Biffl, S. (2006). Optimal Project Feature Weights in analogy-based Cost Estimation: Improvement and Limitations. *IEEE Transactions on Software Engineering*, *32*(2), 83-92.

Waterman, D. A. (2008). *A guide to Expert Systems, First Impression*. Pearson.

Rana, Z. A., Shamail, S., & Awais, M. M. (2007, December). *A Survey of measurement-based software quality prediction techniques* (technical report). Academic Press.

Chapter 5
Software Quality Measures as Degree of Excellence

ABSTRACT

This chapter attempts to develop a system to predict rate of improvement of the software quality at a particular point of time with respect to the number of lines of code present in the software. Having calculated the error level (EL) and degree of excellence (DE) at two points in time, I can move forward towards the estimation of the rate of improvement of the software quality with respect to time. This parameter can be used to judge the amount of effort put into while developing software and can add a new dimension to the understanding of software quality in software engineering domain.

INTRODUCTION

The objective of this chapter is to improve the degree of excellence by removing the number of exceptions from the software. The modern age is more concerned with the quality of software. The rate of improvement of quality of software largely depends on the development time. This development time is chiefly calculated in clock hours. However, development time does not reflect the effort put in by the developer. A better parameter can be the rate of improvement of quality level or the rate of improvement of degree of excellence with respect to time. Now this parameter needs the prediction of error level and degree of excellence at a particular stage of development of the software. This chapter

DOI: 10.4018/978-1-5225-3185-2.ch005

explores an attempt to develop a system to predict rate of improvement of the software quality at a particular point of time with respect to the number of lines of code present in the software (Rashid, Patnaik, & Bhattacherjee, 2014). A machine or algorithm serves its purpose if it fulfills the task of generating quality products in short time. The dream of any engineer is to build machines fitted for this purpose. Researchers have engaged themselves with such tasks and this leads to the development of newer gadgets, devices and machines. Moreover, after the advent of computational machines, the task has also been to develop software that can handle different situations. So, a newer field of research has developed for software development. This field of research grew rapidly over the last decade and many sub-branches have emerged. There is the task of developing new software for newer tasks. Then there is the important area of development of computational languages. Among several others, there is also the need of working with the methodology of software development. This field in particular deals with the notion that what we need should not only be workable software, but should also be efficient. Efficiency amounts to a balance between using the least possible space and employing minimum run-time. So, algorithms and complexity theories emerged rapidly. Then there also emerged the urge to develop tools for programming and thus reducing the workload and stress of both the adept and ordinary programmer. This research work is focused on the two areas. That is, on one hand developing an algorithm that can be used by scientists as well as ordinary programmers to judge and produce software of the best quality, while on the other hand reduce the workload of the man and transfer his burden on the machine (Rashid, Patnaik, & Bhattacherjee, 2012). The main thrust in modern software engineering research is centered on trying to build tools that can enhance software quality. Software quality estimation models in software engineering are used to predict important attributes such as software development effort, software reliability, and productivity of programmers (Bhattacherjee & Kumar, 2005). Software quality prediction is a complex mix of characteristics that varies from application to application and users who request for it. A software quality prediction model can be used to identify the defective modules (Rashid, Patnaik, & Bhattacherjee, 2012). Although cost estimation and quality estimation may have relative independence, the two are dialectically dependent on one another. Cost reduction can be considered to some extent as a parameter of quality. At the same time, quality improvement is sure to affect the cost factor. The cost of software is related to the development time. However, the development time does not truly reflect the effort put in by the developer. A better method is to calculate the rate of improvement of software quality and the effort put in by a developer and to use it as a new parameter to provide a better understanding of the cost of a software. This chapter focuses upon the need and the methods to estimate the rate of improvement of software quality and the effort put in by the developer in the course of software development.

PROBLEM DESCRIPTIONS

The main problem in trying to calculate the rate of improvement of software quality and the effort put in by a developer cannot be measured in a straightforward manner like measuring clocked development time or counting the lines of code. The concept rate of improvement of quality or of effort of development seems to be too abstract as compared to the abovementioned parameters. It has to be understood and defined unambiguously before proceeding further. There may be many arguments and views on the question as to what the term effort actually means and also on what should be the method of its calculations. Nevertheless, a beginning is necessary for refinements to follow. In due course of time, the best understanding may evolve as a result of the collective efforts of many. The problem of estimating the rate of improvement of quality and in due course, calculating the effort as a part of trying to evaluate the cost and the quality of a software makes it necessary to record the history of software development and that too with objective precision. Naturally the question arises as to what is to be recorded? One can record the number of lines of code at a particular instance of time. But this again may not reflect a correct picture of development status. Suppose there are thousands of lines of code with thousands of errors. On the other hand, there may be a few hundred lines of error free code. Quite understandably the thousands of lines of code with as many errors will surely have a much more negative impact on the software development than the few hundreds of lines of error free code. Hence the question of quality of software is somewhat related to the rate of improvement at a particular instance of time. That needs to be correctly ascertained.

The main focus of this work is thus the estimation of the rate of improvement of software quality.

SIGNIFICANCE OF STUDY

- The method of calculation of rate of improvement of quality and in due course the effort estimation as a parameter to calculate the value of the software may develop newer ideas and understanding in the field of software engineering. Treatment of an abstract entity as effort in development may transform to much advanced concepts of what should be the value created by the developer. This may on the one hand decide the developer's merits and strengths while on the other hand may provide a guideline to set a suitable price for the developed software. Although many other factors are inexorably linked in deciding a suitable price for the software, yet the effort parameter shall play no less than a significant role in this regard.

- There is another significance that goes with this study. The calculation of error level and the degree of excellence as an objective measure of the software quality at a particular instance of time is a novel application, unused till date, or at least used very insignificantly. This means an applied form has been successfully evolved from a theoretical construct to enhance the implementation of software engineering concepts.

- Again, the measure of error level and the degree of excellence calls for the deployment of an indigenous tool that can calculate the required statistics accurately and precisely. This again opens up newer vistas in the already vast areas of compiler design and the integration of compiler design into the engineering of automated software. Notwithstanding the indigenous tool again explores further possibilities in this direction.

- This study is also an attempt to explore new data structural designs, which may in future lead to different forms of data structure, hitherto unknown. It may add a new dimension to software engineering concepts, as the software would enable the ordinary programmer generate quality software, the ability of which was confined to only scientist and engineers.

- The quicker development of quality software and the implementation would lead to newer commercial and economic equations. The engineers and the scientific community engaged in developing quality software will be relieved and then they will be able to devote their time to more productive activity, introducing whole new areas for research and knowledge.

ERRORS

Error refers to a condition that creeps in unwanted. It is a mistake committed by a person due to factors which are detrimental to his or her value. It may be lack of concentration, lack of proper training, improper conception of the issue concerned, anxiety, stress and many other factors. Whatever may be the reason, human error is bound to be associated with any piece of work and the conception debugging has actually generated from the understanding that a scientific understanding has to be developed to remove the errors. Now the number of errors that a less experienced person can make is likely to be more that the number of errors likely to be made by a more experienced hand. This brings in the necessity to minimize the number of errors found in any particular piece of work.

WHY TESTING IS IMPORTANT

Due to the activities connected with the fault detection account for a considerable part of the project budget. Examining a Software Module and predicting whether it is faulty or non-faulty. A faulty module is a module which has not passed the certain number of test cases (Rashid, Patnaik, & Bhattacherjee, 2014). I have developed a model for software testing (See Figure 1).

Figure 1. Context-level diagram for testing environment

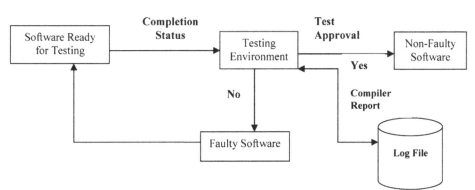

METHODOLOGY

Before going into the methodology, here are some basic definitions and principles (Ben-Menachem & Marliss, 1997):

1. **Error Level (EL):** The error level of software at a particular instance of time with respect to the number of lines of code (LOC) is defined as the ratio of the number of errors detected to the number of lines of code at that particular instance of time.

$$EL = \frac{\text{number of errors detected}}{\text{number of LOC}} \qquad (1)$$

Now this ratio when expressed in percentage gives the percentage error level.

2. **Degree of Excellence (X):** The Degree of Excellence of software at a particular instance of time with respect to the number of lines of code is defined as the ratio of the correct number of lines of code to the total number of lines of code expressed in percentage.

Thus:

$$X = 100 - EL\% \qquad (2)$$

3. **Improvement of Degree of Excellence:** The improvement of the Degree of Excellence of software may be defined as the difference between the Degrees of Excellence between two points of time.

Thus:

$$\text{Improvement} = X_f - X_i \qquad (3)$$

where X_f and X_i stand for final Degree of Excellence and initial degree of Excellence between two points of time.

4. **Rate of Improvement of Software Quality:** It can be easily understood that once the developer or the team of developers has been decided upon

the parameter X (Degree of Excellence) is just a function of time. And then I can define the rate of improvement of software quality as:

The rate of improvement of software quality is the derivative of the degree of excellence with respect to time.

With this understanding the following principle can be stated:

5. **Principle of Effort in Software Development:** The principle of effort in software development states that – 'The effort put in software development is proportional to the rate of improvement of degree of excellence of the software with respect to time.'

Thus:

$$E \propto \frac{dX}{dt} \tag{4}$$

or

$$E = \alpha \frac{dX}{dt} \tag{5}$$

where α is the constant of proportionality and may be called the coefficient of the developer's ability.

The methodology involved is the following:

•   Using an indigenous tool, we first calculate the error level and degree of excellence at two different points of time.
•   Then the improvement of the degree of excellence and subsequently the rate of improvement of the degree of excellence can be calculated in the methods mentioned above.
•   If the improvement of the degree of excellence is expressed as a function of time, then the effort in software development at a particular instance of time can be calculated as the derivative of the degree of excellence with respect to time at that particular point of time.
•   The indigenous tool uses 'C' as the programming language.

ANALYSIS AND RESULTS

The aim of this research was to identify the number of errors in the software as well as total number of loops used in the software like for loop, while loop. The objective was to test the software, whether the software is faulty or non-faulty. Quality level or degree of excellence was calculated on the basis of error level with respect to lines of code found in the software. In order to obtain the results the indigenous tool has been used.

The tool was working as (Rashid, Patnaik, & Bhattacherjee, 2014):

1. The tool asks for the file which contains the code and after that has been provided,
2. The tool scans for the number of lines of code (LOC) excluding comments line in the software after that is done,
3. The tool asks for the name of the log file which contains the error report of the compiler.
4. After the name of the log file has been provided, the tool searches for the number of errors in the log file and then calculates the degree of excellence as well as the error level of the code at the particular instance of time and gives the output (See Figure 2 through Figure 3).

The output can be noted down and a graph can be prepared as shown below. The different types of graph forms show uniform or constant improvement,

Figure 2. Quality level or degree of excellence of a file with no error is 100%

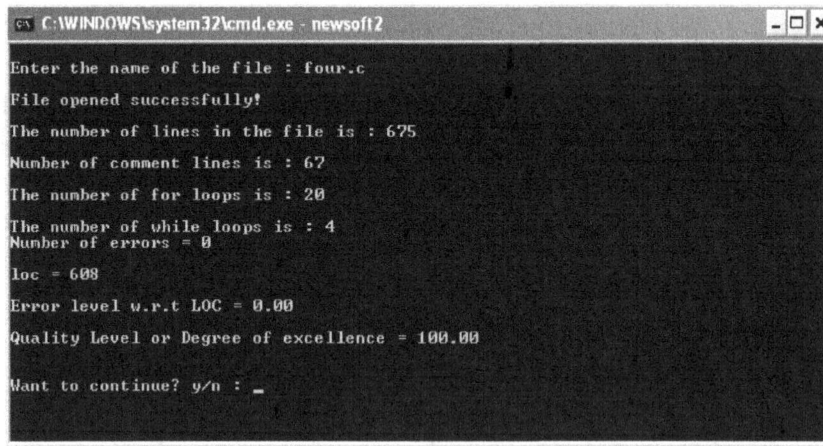

Figure 3. Analysis of file with eight errors, quality level, or degree of excellence 99.15%

C:\WINDOWS\system32\cmd.exe - newsoft2
Enter the name of the file : exponent.c
File opened successfully!
The number of lines in the file is : 1117
Number of comment lines is : 173
The number of for loops is : 27
The number of while loops is : 4
Number of errors = 8
loc = 944
Error level w.r.t LOC = 0.85
Quality Level or Degree of excellence = 99.15
Want to continue? y/n :

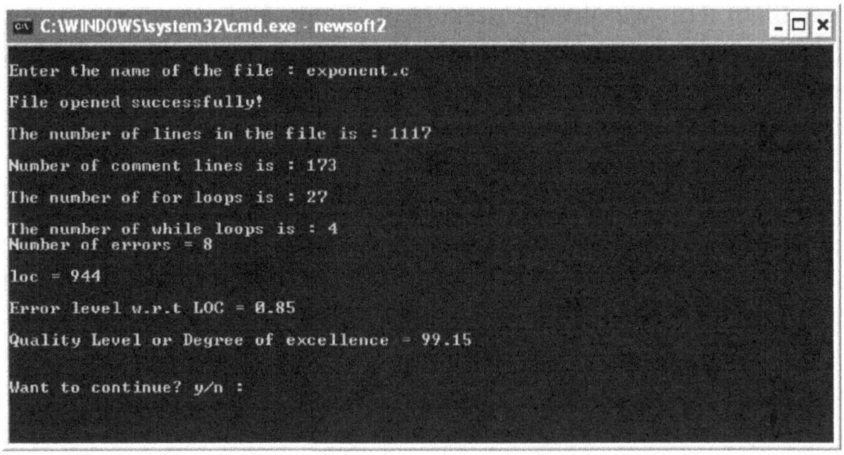

positive improvement and negative improvement respectively. The slope of the secant of the graph at any two points of time gives the average improvement between those two points in time while the tangent at any point gives the instantaneous rate of improvement at any particular instance of time shown in Figure 4.

Figure 4. Degree of excellence with respect to time

Degree of Excellence
8
7
6
5
4
3
2
1
0
1 unit
2 units
3 units
4 units
5 units
6 units
constant improvement
positive improvement
negative improvement
Time

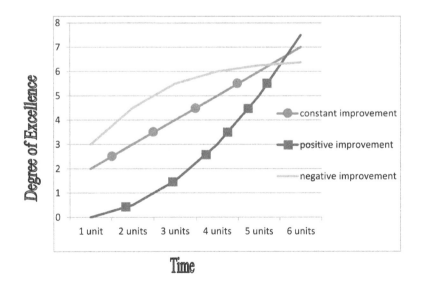

CONCLUSION

The calculation of rate of improvement of quality and effort in the software development may add new dimensions to the understanding of software engineering. This research work will be expanded to include newer concepts on the basis of the understanding of rate of improvement of quality and effort in software development which no longer remains an abstract term but on the contrary, becomes a true quantity that can be measured, estimated and compared at different levels. The knowledge about the rate of improvement of software quality and effort in software development, leads us to the correct estimation of the quality of the software and also the quality of the developer. The price of the software can be ascertained more precisely as a result.

REFERENCES

Ben-Menachem, M., & Marliss, G. S. (1997). *Software Quality: Producing Practical, Consistent Software*. New Delhi: Vikas Publishing House.

Bhattacherjee, V., & Kumar, S. (2005). Software cost estimation and its relevance in the Indian software Industry. *Proceedings of the International Conference on Emerging Technologies IT Industry*.

Rashid, E., & Patnaik, S., & Bhattacherjee, V. (2012). A Survey in the Area of Machine Learning and Its Application for Software Quality Prediction. *ACM SigSoft Software Engineering Notes*, *37*(5). doi:10.1145/2347696.2347709

Rashid, E., Patnaik, S., & Bhattacherjee, V. (2012). Strategies Towards Improving Software Code Quality in Computing. *International Journal of Engineering Research and Applications*, *2*(3), 2253–2257.

Rashid, E., Patnaik, S., & Bhattacherjee, V. (2014). Prediction of rate of Improvement of Software Quality and Development Effort on the Basis of Degree of Excellence with respect to Number of Lines of Code. *International Journal of Computer Engineering and Applications*, *5*(3), 6–13.

Chapter 6
Understanding the State of Quality of Software

ABSTRACT

The effort of this chapter is directed towards introducing a new mathematical model to understand the state of quality of software by calculating parameters such as the time gap and quality gap with relation to some predefined standard software quality or in relation to some chalked out software quality plan. This chapter deals about the status of the quality of the software that is being developed. This chapter also indicates methods to calculate the difference in the quality of the software being developed and the model software which has been decided upon as the criteria for comparison. These methods will provide a better understanding of quality as compared to other standards.

INTRODUCTION

This research work suggests a new mathematical model to understand the state of quality of software by calculating parameters such as the time gap and quality gap with relation to some predefined standard software quality or in relation to some chalked out software quality plan. The chapter also suggests methods to calculate the difference in the quality of the software being developed and the model software which has been decided upon as the criteria for comparison (Rashid, Patnaik, & Bhattacherjee, 2013).

Quality is not an absolute term. Rather, just like other scientific parameters, it should be viewed as something relative, precise and concrete. Even the

DOI: 10.4018/978-1-5225-3185-2.ch006

measurement of quality has to be contemplated with the correct approach, which is on the basis of comparison with some specific standard. For instance, what do we mean when I say that something is five meters long. Obviously, I have some standard length, which we call one meter, and when compared to that, my object in discussion is five times that standard lengths. Similar is the case of measuring other scientific parameters. The comparisons are made with some specific standards which are globally recognized. However, in the case of software engineering, quality measures do not have globally recognized concrete values. There are sets of standards defined by the IEEE as to how a software quality should be estimated. Only when some concrete software has been identified as the measuring standard, can I precisely calculate the quality of any software by comparing it to that given standard. This chapter outlines the possible comparison parameters to understand the state of quality of software on the basis of such a comparison. The parameters that have been used are novel ideas and have not been previously used in the realm of software engineering. Moreover, an attempt has been made to chalk out a mathematical model, and a concrete strategy so as to precisely determine the quality of the software being developed. As elucidated earlier, the basis of quality determination is chiefly by drawing out an analogy between what is being developed and what is already developed. Although the author considers that an international standard has to be established, regarding this quality, unless that is achieved, I can define my own standards in my own institutes and organizations and use the methods given herewith to determine concretely the state of quality of the software being developed. The mathematical methods employed are very basic and can be used by any ordinary person. The parameters and terms may be enriched and advanced to form newer concepts and ideas. On the whole after the required comparisons have been made and the particular understanding of the quality has been achieved, decisions can be taken suitably to augment the proper and rapid quality software development.

RELATED WORKS

Whenever I talk about quality, I talk about the defects in the software. So, the method of determining the quality of a software is inexorably linked to the ideal of software testing. There are many methods employed in software testing such as – on the basis of thousand lines of code, on the basis of per hundred hours of development time, on the basis of per hundred tests conducted

(Srinivasan & Gopalaswamy, 2012). There are works regarding the technique and framework to measure the quality of software. This technique leverages technology that automatically analyzes 100% of the paths through a given code base, thus allowing a consistent examination of every possible outcome when running the resulting software. Using this new approach to measuring quality, there has been a target to give visibility into how various open source projects, compare to each other and suggest a new way to make software better (Chelf, 2006). There have been studies where the research objective is to build a parametric model which utilizes a persistent record of the validation and verification (V&V) practices used with a program to estimate the defect density of that program. The persistent record of the V&V practices is recorded as certificates which are automatically recorded and maintained with the code (Sherriff & Williams, 2006). There has been the attempt to make an analogy-based software quality estimation with project feature weights. The objective of such research is to predict the quality of the project accurately and use the results in future predictions (Rashid, Patnaik, & Bhattacharya, 2013). In-process quality metrics are less formally defined than end-product metrics, and their practices vary greatly among software developers. On the one hand, in-process quality metrics simply means tracking, defect arrival during formal machine testing for some organizations. On the other hand, some software organizations with well-established software metrics programs cover various parameters in each phase of the development cycle (Kan, 2002). It is especially in the context of the last idea that this research work has been designed. The target is to achieve the quality during the development process and that has been explained in the section of objectives as below.

OBJECTIVE

The objective of this research is to calculate precisely the status of the software during the course of its development. This objective is further linked to the focus of trying to analyze whether the development process is on the right track. If the development process is not proceeding as per the expected lines, corrective or remedial measures may be undertaken to bring it back on the desired track. The concrete quality measurement is not the quality of the end product. Rather, it is the quality of the software at various stages. Normally, the final quality is talked about more in the domain of software engineering. However, I have to understand that the final quality can only be achieved if the intermediate quality levels are assured. Especially if I follow a model of software development, such as the Boehm's spiral model, where there are consistent checks at regular stages to see if the software is developed on the required lines or not, the method given in the present chapter will prove to be very useful. This method will also prove to be effective in all forms of iterative models of software development. The chapter also fulfills the objective of defining the necessary metrics to make the above measurements. A new idea is certainly accompanied by newer metrics. If one has to use these ideas, that brings them into proper application, he/she has to make use of the newer metrics. However, they have to be understood in connection to other metrics. So, all the metrics that have been used in this chapter have been defined and their significance explained therein. This chapter also has the objective to present an alternative mathematical model and a very simple one so as to enable the organizations to take decisions in the right direction.

METHODOLOGY

The measurement of software quality has been done on an analogy basis. The environment of our study is the college campus and our target group is the B. Tech students of computer science and engineering. Students are guided with their project supervisor, supported by the technical staffs, resources like computers, software etc. The quality values for software being developed were given by the supervisor on the basis of performance of the students during development of the projects in month wise. The project duration was a period of one year. The following gives the steps in the process:

1. First, there should be a quality function related to the type of software being developed. This quality function should be a function of time. This quality function can be decided either by any international body (only then can the measurement be universalized) or by any organization interested in determining the quality of the software at various phases of software development. To put it more elaborately, I can have a separate quality function for a particular type of software. To decide what this quality function should be, one has to go back and trace the history of the development of similar types of software developed in accordance with the principles and methods laid out in the IEEE standards. The quality function can be linear or polynomial depending upon the complexity of the software and upon the known history of its development. How does one arrive at this function? I have shown the method to arrive at such a

standard function by using some synthetic data. Let us assume for the sake of simplicity that it takes twelve months to develop some typical software and the quality measured in the range 1-12 of the software developed is as shown below (See Table 1).

Figure 1 has shown quality vs time with the help of the data shown in Table 1.

Table 1. Synthetic datasets (quality vs. time)

Time (in Months)	Quality
1	5
2	8
3	11
4	14
5	17
6	20
7	23
8	26
9	29
10	32
11	35
12	38

Figure 1. Quality vs. time

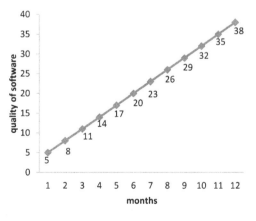

graph of quality versus time

The quality function then can be easily determined which will be as under for the given data. This function can be decided by the individual or organization that is going to develop the software based on previous experiences.

$$Q(t) = 3t + 2 \tag{1}$$

where

Q = Quality function

t = Time in months

2.   Next, after close monitoring, I have framed the check point months wise when software is being developed by the B. Tech students of computer science in group. The project name was "Software Quality Assurance in XP Model". In this case, I am using student's data after checking the quality value achieved by the students in every month with respect to standard software. On the basis of the data for the software being developed, I can plot the points on the same graph. There is less possibility that this graph will be linear or of any regular form. The quality of software being developed is improving as per the following data (See Table 2).

Table 2. Real data set (quality vs. time)

Time (in Months)	Quality
1	3
2	6
3	8
4	9
5	10
6	13
7	14
8	17
9	20
10	22
11	25
12	27

On the basis of the data shown in Table 2, we can plot a graph shown in Figure 2.

3. Next, I calculate the quality gap. For this, at a particular point of time I identify the quality of the standard software (q1) and then from the graph of the standard software I draw a line vertically from that point to reach the graph of the software being developed. I then identify the quality of the software being developed (q2) corresponding to this point. Then the relation q1 – q2 gives the quality gap. As an example, I have taken the above data to calculate the quality gap between the software being developed and the standard software available with us for comparison. Iare calculating the quality gap just after six months of software development work has been completed. I can also do the same from the data given. I see that the quality of the standard software at six-month time point is 20 while the software being developed has reached quality of 13 after six months. Then I can say that the quality gap at six months is 7. This fact is being illustrated in Figure 3 and 4, respectively.

4. Next, I calculate the time gap. In order to calculate the time gap, I first pick a particular quality value of the standard software for which I want to calculate the time gap. Next, I identify the time (t1) at which the standard software had acquired that quality and also the point on the graph of the standard software corresponding to that particular

Figure 2. Quality vs. time

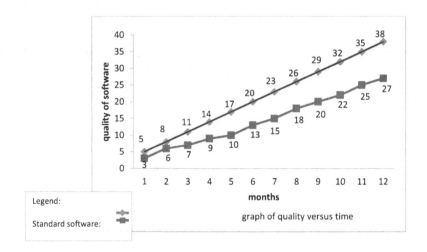

Figure 3. Quality gap

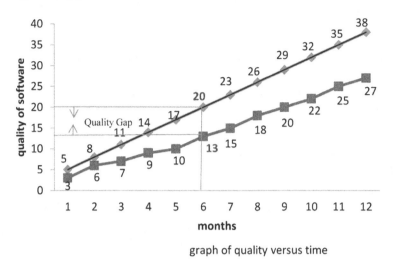

quality of software
40
35
30
25
20
15
10
5
0
Quality Gap
5 8 11 14 17 20 23 26 29 32 35 38
3 6 7 9 10 13 15 18 20 22 25 27
1 2 3 4 5 6 7 8 9 10 11 12
months
graph of quality versus time

Figure 4. Measuring the quality gap after six months

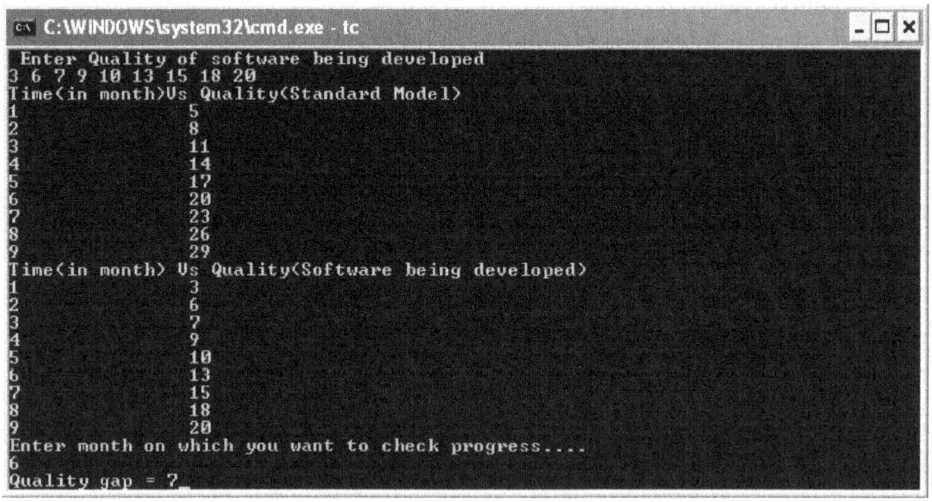

C:\WINDOWS\system32\cmd.exe - tc
Enter Quality of software being developed
3 6 7 9 10 13 15 18 20
Time(in month)Vs Quality(Standard Model)
1 5
2 8
3 11
4 14
5 17
6 20
7 23
8 26
9 29
Time(in month) Vs Quality(Software being developed)
1 3
2 6
3 7
4 9
5 10
6 13
7 15
8 18
9 20
Enter month on which you want to check progress....
6
Quality gap = 7

quality. I then draw a horizontal line to meet the graph of the software being developed. Where the line meets the graph of the software being developed, I identify the corresponding time (t2). Then t1 – t2 gives the time gap between the two for the particular stage of quality. As, for example, we have identified the time when the standard software acquires the quality 20 as 6 months. For the same quality I see that the software being developed is taking 9 months. So, for the quality level 20, I say that the time gap is 3 months. This fact has been illustrated in Figure 5 and 6, respectively. The time gap between the standard software and the software being developed has been shown illustratively. In the same manner, we can tabulate a series of data showing the quality gap at a particular time of software development and the time gap at a particular level of quality as parameters of comparison.

5. The difference between the standard software and the software being developed can be found out about the concept of the Euclidian distance or the Manhattan distance. For this I first identify two points in the two graphs. I simply use the x and y coordinates of the two points and the understanding of distance between two points in a Cartesian plane to find the difference between the two points. The expressions for calculating the distance between the two points are as given below:

$$\text{dist}\ (p_1, p_2) = [(x_2\text{-}x_1)^2 + (y_2\text{-}y_1)^2]^{1/2} \tag{2}$$

A small distance indicates a high degree of similarity (Rashid, Patnaik, & Bhattacharya, 2013). Similarly, a bigger distance indicates a larger difference between the two.

The difference between the two points in the example being used here is shown in the following illustration. See Figure 7.

Figure 5. Time gap

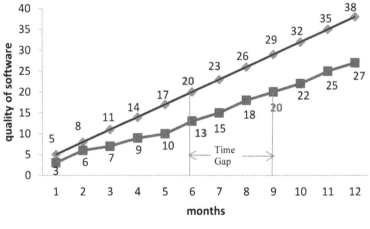

graph of quality versus time

Figure 6. Measuring the time gap after six months

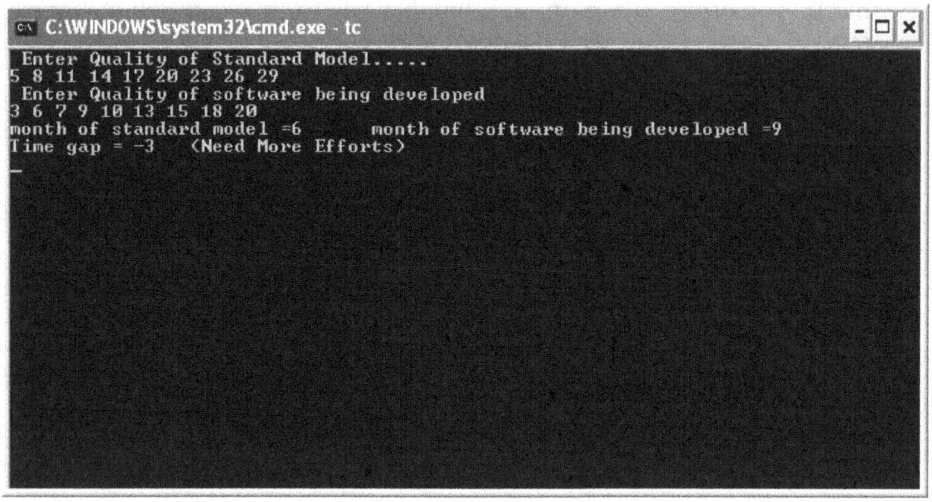

```
C:\WINDOWS\system32\cmd.exe - tc                                    - □ ×
 Enter Quality of Standard Model.....
5 8 11 14 17 20 23 26 29
 Enter Quality of software being developed
3 6 7 9 10 13 15 18 20
month of standard model =6        month of software being developed =9
Time gap = -3   (Need More Efforts)
_
```

Figure 7. Synthetic datasets (distance between two points in a Cartesian plane)

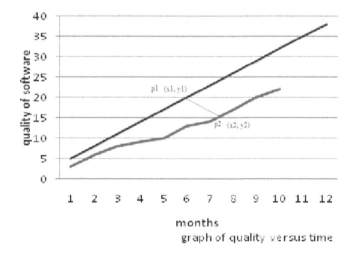

ANALYSIS AND RESULTS

On the basis of the above parameters I can estimate the direction which the software being developed is taking. This will help us estimate the state of the quality of the software being developed. The quality gap between the standard software and the software being developed helps us to understand how much more effort needs to be put in terms of removing defects and improving code quality. More the quality gap, more is the amount of effort needed to be put in this regard. The time gap between the standard software and the software being developed shows us how much the software being developed is lagging behind the standard software in terms of time. More the time gap, the more is the effort needed in terms of quickening the process of software development. If necessary, the number of software development personnel has to be increased in order to match the standard quality. In this way, we can say that the quality gap speaks qualitatively about the software. The quality of the software developers has to be improved to bridge that gap. On the other hand, the time gap speaks quantitatively about the software. The number of software developers needs to be increased in order to bridge the gap with respect to the standard software. The difference between the standard software and the software being developed gives the overall view about the status of the quality of the software being developed. It helps us in understanding the overall effort needed in terms of achieving a particular quality of standard software. See Table 3.

CONCLUSION

This chapter deals about the status of the quality of the software that is being developed. The importance of the work lies in the fact that the parameters that have been introduced here give a clear picture about the qualitative and the quantitative states of the software stage. The parameters can be used for other kinds of software analysis as determining how much effort needs to be put in as regards to which aspect to improve the quality of the software. Only when I compare the software with any particular standard can this be made possible. For this reason I stress upon the necessity of having an international standard of various types of software that are typically being developed nowadays.

Table 3. Summary of standard software and software being developed

Quality of Standard Software (Six Months)	Quality of Software Being Developed (Six Months)	Quality of Software Being Developed (Nine Months)	Quality Gap Between Standard Software and Software Being Developed (20-13) (Six months)	Time Gap Between Standard Software and Software Being Developed (9-6)
20	13	20	7	3

It would be better to express the standards as functions of time so that the comparisons can be easily made. The concepts used here are significant as they can be further enhanced to develop newer understandings about the quality. Here I have taken the development time in terms of number of months. For smaller software, I can take the development time in terms of number of days. I can also review the concept by using a number of software developers instead of taking the number of months for software development. Then I shall be calculating some other parameters instead of time gap, but then the parameter quality gap would remain. Only this time it would be in terms of number of working hands instead of being calculated with respect to time.

REFERENCES

Chelf, B. (2006). *Measuring software quality, a study of open source software*. Coverity, Inc.

Rashid, E., & Patnaik, S., & Bhattacherjee, V. (2013a). Understanding the State of Quality of Software on the basis of Time Gap, Quality Gap and Difference with Standard Model. *International Journal of Engineering and Technology*, *5*(3), 2821-2827.

Rashid, E., Patnaik, S., & Bhattacharya, V. (2013b). Analogy-based Software Quality Prediction with Project Feature Weights. *American Journal of Software Engineering and Applications*, *2*(2), 49–53. doi:10.11648/j.ajsea

Kan, S. H. (2002). *Metrics and Models in Software Quality Engineering* (2nd ed.). New Delhi, India: Pearson Education.

Sherriff, M., & Williams, L. (2006). *Defect Density Estimation Through Verification and Validation*. North Carolina State University Raleigh.

Srinivasan, D., & Gopalaswamy, R. (2012). *Software Testing, Principles and Practices*. Pearson Education.

Chapter 7

Estimation and Evaluation of Software Quality at a Particular Stage of Software Development

ABSTRACT

In this chapter, some new ideas about estimation and evaluation of the quality of software. At the outset, it deals with the possibilities of using a standard conversion method so that lines of code from any language may be compared and be used as a uniform metric. The present work is also credited through the introduction of some new terms like efficiency and variation to understand the change in software quality. The main focus is to evaluate and estimate software quality at a particular stage of software development. This is not average quality understanding, but quality estimation at a particular instance. One of the salient aspects of the method suggested is that the developer can evaluate the work at any stage using the methods given to review the present status and make future plans to meet the required target.

INTRODUCTION

This research work suggests a method of comparing the actual rate of software development with the projected or targeted rate. The actual rate of software development can be calculated at a particular stage of work and the required comparisons can be made (Rashid, Patnaik, & Bhattacherjee, 2013). It is

DOI: 10.4018/978-1-5225-3185-2.ch007

very common to see large projects being undertaken at the present time. The software being developed in such projects goes through many phases of development and can be very complicated in terms of quality assessment. There will always be a concern for proper quality and effective cost estimation of such software. This can be rather tricky as the project being a large one may cover several unknown and unseen factors that might previously be very difficult to judge. The pertinent question here is how can I judge in case of such a large project, whether the progress that is being made at a particular stage of software development is really up to the mark. How can I be assured that the rate of development of quality of the software at a particular stage is actually satisfactory enough? This analysis becomes more important because there is every possibility of losing out in the midst of development work without proper scientific planning and evaluation methods. It may so happen that the subjective understanding of the progress in development may lead to unexpected results. This will surely affect the ultimate cost and the quality of the software. At the same time one can easily understand that the result of the efforts may be totally disastrous. More the scientific approach in this regard, better is the possibility of achieving expected results. It would be best if a proper mathematical model is available to assess and compare the rate of development of software at a particular stage of development. With properly defined steps and methods, it would be easy to draw correct and objective conclusions. In this method, subjective analysis will be replaced by proper scientific assessment. This chapter suggests the steps and the proper methods to be followed for this kind of activity. The novelty in this approach is the use of differential calculus to obtain the correct quantitative analysis. The quantitative analysis itself is a form of qualitative analysis with the help of which proper decisions may be taken to make up for any losses or lacunas in the development work. Simultaneously, there may also be the possibility of over usage of resources, that is, resources that are being used, but, are not really required. Due to lack of understanding about the correct rate of development at various stages, organizations may tend to over use their resources, when then could do with lesser options. The assessment of quality at different stages with the help of the methods given in this chapter and their proper records would create an important statistical knowledgebase which would result in better understanding of the life cycle of any typical software type. Division of work and allocating the number of workers per module will be easier than before. When software is being developed, the development team has to be focused on the quality of the software and also on the cost involved. The cost factor is more or less measurable and has well defined metrics. There are different models which can help us estimate the cost of software. The chief among them are: The cost involves calculating parameters such as lines of code and effort. There has been a detailed analysis of estimating the effort and also tried to elucidate the rate of improvement of software quality with respect to time. Several calculations such as the time derivative of improvement of quality and other metrics have been discussed in (Rashid, Patnaik, & Bhattacherjee, 2014). This has to do chiefly with deciding the quality of the software, which has been by and large believed to be a much more subjective issue when compared to the estimation of cost. Whenever the quality issue is involved, we have to view in perspective of its explanations and definitions as put forward by the authorities over the subject. Let us at the outset, mention in brief the understanding involved about quality decision. Every software requirement specification document has a set of functional requirements stated therein. Now these explicitly stated functional requirements need to be fulfilled and the degree to which they are fulfilled can be understood as the quality of the software. Moreover, there is also a set of implicit requirements that the development team needs to enumerate. These sets of implicit functional requirements also need to be fulfilled for getting the quality software. Another view that defines the quality of software is as follows: Quality achievement is a state in which the software becomes free from bugs, meets the cost factors, can be developed within the stipulated time frame and has an overall controlled time and space complexity. However, this can be argued to be more or less the viewpoint of the developer. For the end user, quality largely refers to that condition of software where it is "working", is reasonable "fast", is quite "user friendly" and is "easily upgradable". Thus the status of the person getting involved with respect to the software largely determines the issue of the conception of software quality. This research work is an attempt to improve upon the earlier conception of software development by defining some new metrics. This part focuses on the development period of the software and has little to do with the quality of the final product. On the other side, the new parameters introduced in the chapter, aim towards deciding upon the quality at the end of the software development. Both the issues largely reflect the work of software quality estimation and may be considered to be important in many respects as mentioned in the subsequent sections.

RELATED WORK AND MOTIVATION

There are already several well-defined attributes for quality testing. The most prominent among them are: Auditability, compatibility, completeness, consistency, correctness, feasibility, modularity, predictability, robustness, structuredness, testability, traceability, understandability, verifiability, etc. Some of the well-defined metrics to be measured in different stages of software development are defect metrics and maintainability metrics. The intrinsic product quality is generally measured by identifying the number of 'bugs' in the software or by measuring how long the software can run before encountering a 'crash'. In operational definition, the two are termed as defect density rate and the mean time to failure (MTTF). The two metrics are correlated but are different enough to merit close attention. First, one measures the time between failures, the other measures the defects relative to the software size (lines of code, function points, etc.) (Kan, 2002). This brings back the discussion on the differences between the terms error, fault, defect and failure. According to the IEEE/ ANSI standard:

- An error is a human mistake that results in incorrect software.
- The resulting fault is an accidental condition that causes a unit of the system to fail to function as required.
- A defect is an anomaly in a product.
- A failure occurs when a functional unit of a software-related system can no longer perform its required function or cannot perform it within specified limits (IEEE/American National Standards Institute [ANSI] standard [982.2]).

However, as pointed out by noted authorities on the subject, there is not much difference to be made between fault and defect and one can observe that these terms are used interchangeably in the industry. Over and above it has been felt that the terms defect or fault may be used with the end product while the term error may be used during the development process. This means that the term error refers to the mistake made by the developer and may be considered to be unintended or accidental. On the contrary, the terms defect or fault may refer to some anomaly or inadequacy in the entire software itself, which points towards the fact that the designer was unable to foresee potential problems in advance. So, the term defect density deals with the end product and so does the term MTTF. However, there should be a term to determine the quality at each stage of development of the software. In such cases, there can be a term used often called code quality which is normally referred to as the ratio of the number of lines of code to the number of defects in the program. When there is a mention about using the number of lines of code, it becomes incumbent to mention the different viewpoints regarding the issue of counting lines of code or LOC as it is abbreviated.

The following can be taken as an authoritative definition of LOC:

A line of code is any line of program text that is not a comment or blank line, regardless of the number of statements or fragments of statements on the line. This specifically includes all lines containing program headers, declarations, and executable and non-executable statements. (Conte et al., 1986)

This was the definition from Conte. Now another established authority on the subject, Boehm says the LOC counting method counts lines as physical lines and includes executable lines, data definitions, and comments (Boehm, 1981). There is also the issue of counting the physical and the logical LOC. It is widely opined that the counting of logical LOC is a better choice for quality data. However, there are several problems in this field as programming is done in different languages and so it is difficult to strike uniformity. While assembly language may need much more lines of code as compared to high level languages, an object-oriented language (OOL) may have totally different paradigms for coding as compared to structured programming language. There is the idea of converting the code into equivalent lines of assembly code. For this the LOC counted on the basis of some agreed standard is multiplied with some coefficient or some ratio to get the normalized value. For this purpose, the table of conversion values published by Jones in 1986 is the most popular in the industry today. In addition to this there may be other standards that can be adopted by different organizations from time to time. Whatever be the set of standards adopted, it is necessary to specify them and then do the remaining calculation.

SIGNIFICANCE

The significance of this study is manifold. The following can be shortlisted as some important points:

1. The greatest problem faced by analysts while dealing with lines of code is that they are not able to compare the coding is done in different

programming languages. Once a common parameter or coefficient is set, and the code from any programming language can be converted into its assembly equivalent or into any other form that can make it comparable to code of other languages in any standard form, the problem faced with the issue of LOC becomes solved. This will make the work of analysis straightforward and may remove the different complicacies involved in the process.

2. The improvement of code quality with respect to the time given for development work is yet another parameter. If assessed and measured correctly, it can not only decide the proper cost of the software, but also ascertain the value of the developer. Besides, as the development work progresses, if we are able to determine the rate of improvement of code quality, then we can also have an alternative assessment of the quality of the final product. This will be a novel idea in the realm of software engineering.

3. The introduction of a new attribute of software quality can help one understand the software better. After all what is the significance of any quality attributes? The significance lies in the fact that more the number of attributes, the better we can understand the issue. Hence it is better to introduce more attributes so that the issue of software quality can be understood meticulously and with greater effect. Here it also needs mention that a new attribute can bring into effect understanding of newer terms which on the whole can enrich the literature of the subject.

4. As already mentioned earlier, when we are assessing the quality of both the development phase of the software as well as the quality of the end product, I am establishing a dialectical relationship between the two. For it becomes very obvious that if the rate of improvement of the software is higher, the end product has to be of a much higher quality. Conversely, if the quality of the end product is high, it means that the rate of improvement of the quality of the software must have been quite significant. So, goes the dialectical relationship.

5. So, this work is significant not only because it introduces additional methods for the quality assessment of the end product, but it is also important because while trying to calculate the rate of improvement of code quality with respect to development time, I can predict the quality of the end product at any particular stage of software development. This means that I am working towards a specific goal in terms of achieving the software quality. The assessment of the end product must not vary

in great detail from the prediction made in this manner. This is totally a new concept in the field of software engineering.

Looking from the other way, once I have a final product, I can also guess what should be the improvement rate of the software product at any particular stage given the fact, as it is also mentioned in point IV that the two are related dialectically to each other and as mentioned in point V, I can go to the bottom up approach, and software development like all other natural laws loves symmetry, implying that when I can go bottom up, I can also have a top down approach with things.

METHODOLOGY

As software develops from an initial stage to higher stages, it undergoes several changes. A proper planning can take it to improved levels and higher quality. However, this continuous improvement of quality and standard cannot be achieved without a conscious and diligent effort. Moreover, hard work and pious wishes cannot bring about the improvement of quality. This has brought about the theories of software engineering and has largely transformed a practice that was much more like an art to an activity that has the closest relationship towards scientific methodology. This has brought about the recipes needed to bring out the product in right time and with the right quality. Although many methods and means already exist and continuous research is available in this field, things are not such that we have had enough and that in spite of all the knowledge in this domain things are not in wanting.

Rather more the amount of research being performed in this area, more are things getting better, clear and precise. This rightly reflects the philosophical fact that truth is indeed concrete, particular and precise. Therefore, this research has also worked upon the different phases of software development in order to ascertain the improvement of quality at each level of development. This means that during the development of the software, I need to be sure that the software being developed is actually going in the right direction. And this determination must not be based on just subjective formulations, but on objective figures and facts. It has to be established on specific models and metrics. There should be measured parameters that can serve as indicators of growth or decay. These are the factors that need to be defined, understood, and established with a view to achieving the required goal. With this objective of studying and estimating the improvement of quality of software during the development phase the following are some of the different terms and definitions related to the same:

- **LOC:** The lines of code continue to be the determining metric in most of the quality and cost measurement. Now the method in which the LOC count has to be taken is also not standardized as yet. However, if I for the sake of simplicity assume that a standardization has been achieved, then on the basis of those set standards, after taking the LOC count, I can normalize the same as below:

Let the number of coded lines in assembly language be n.

Let the number of coded lines in any particular language be N. Now it is obvious that more the number of coded lines in any particular high level language, more will be the number of coded lines for the corresponding program in assembly. Hence, I can say that,

$$n \propto N \tag{1}$$

Meaning that as the number of lines in the assembly level language is directly proportional to the number of lines in the concerned high level language.

Now let the standard coefficient for the particular high level language be k.

This coefficient will be the one decided according to the IEEE/ANSI standard. Then the final normalized equivalent lines of code in the assembly will be given by:

$$n = kN \tag{2}$$

where n now denotes the normalized value of the equivalent lines of code in the assembly language. Now this normalized value for the number of lines of code can be used to calculate the cost of the software or the quality of the software as required.

This standard LOC count after being normalized serves as the primary metric.

- **Development Time:** The development time can also be a confusing factor. With experienced personnel, the development time is sure to be on the lower side. However, if the staff is not equipped enough, I am going to have a prolonged development time with respect to any particular work. The development time can be calculated on the basis of man hours, or working days or months. This largely depends upon the nature of the organization and the type of software being developed. At this juncture, I can only say that lesser the unit of development time, the greater is the accuracy of estimation of the quality of product. Errors: The number of errors is also dependent on the person or the team of persons developing the software. If the developers are experienced there are lesser chances of errors. There may be exceptions to this. However, this is the normal trend. Similarly, the errors may increase if the staff is relatively inexperienced. Moreover, there is also the issue of debugging. It becomes very difficult to debug the software if the staff is not experienced. On the other hand, experienced and skilled developers can debug programs more efficiently.

This takes us towards the calculation of the rate of change of software quality. The rate of change of software quality can be calculated in two ways:

1. With respect to time
2. With respect to LOC

The rate of change of software quality with respect to time can be defined as the following:

The average change rate in software quality with respect to time is the change in the software quality per unit development time.

Let the initial software quality be q_i and the final software quality be q_f. Then the change in software quality becomes $q_f - q_i$.

The rate of change of software quality with respect to LOC can be defined as the following:

The average change rate in software quality with respect to LOC is the change in the software quality per line of code where the total lines of code have been taken in the normalized form. Both these concepts are further mathematically formulated in the next section.

RESULTS AND ANALYSIS: THE VARIATION

In the previous section the concept of average rate of change of quality with respect to time and the LOC has been explained. Since this parameter is expected to play a pivotal role in the estimation of software quality, it becomes incumbent to associate a name to it. The name that seems to be fit for the concept is *variation*.

The average rate of change of software quality can be termed asan average variation of software.

From the previous section, we can reformulate as under:

1. With respect to development time:

$$\text{Average Variation} = \frac{q_f - q_i}{\text{development time}} \tag{3}$$

2. With respect to LOC:

$$\text{Average Variation} = \frac{q_f - q_i}{L_f - L_i} \tag{4}$$

Where the symbols have the following meanings:

* q_f = final quality
* q_i = initial quality
* L_f = final normalized LOC
* L_i = initial normalized LOC

When I think in terms of the software quality, the average variation geometrically represents the slope of the secant joining two points in the graph of quality versus time. The figure 1 below is the case of particular software with some synthetic data showing how an increase in quality of software looks geometrically when plotted against time. See table 1.

Figure 1 has shown quality vs. time with the help of Table 1.

Now when I calculate the average variation between two stages of development of the software, namely P and Q, what I get is the slope of the line PQ. The line PQ is shown in the next figure. It joins the points P and Q. This forms the basis on which the concept of instantaneous variation is to be developed. Here it needs to be noted that this average variation is between

Table 1. Synthetic datasets (quality vs. time)

Time	Quality
1 unit	0.5
2 unit	0.6
3 unit	0.9
4 unit	1.5
5 unit	2.7
6 unit	5.1
7 unit	9.9
8 unit	19.5

Figure 1. Quality vs. time

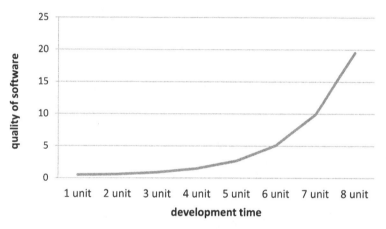

graph of quality versus time

time 3 unit to 7 unit. Had the development been as calculated in the average variation, it would have reached the same level in the particular stage Q. See Figure 2.

However, it becomes more useful if an instantaneous rate is calculated. That actually enables the developer or anyone concerned to understand whether the software is being developed in the right direction and in proper pace at any particular stage, both from the viewpoint of time and also from the viewpoint of LOC.I have seen earlier that the average rate of change

Figure 2. Quality vs. time

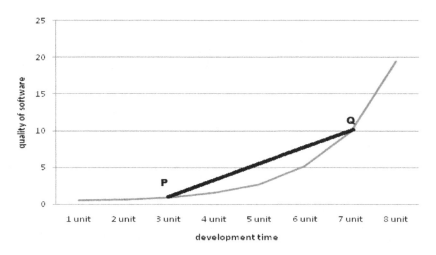

graph of quality versus time

of software quality can be termed as an average variation of software. On the other hand, the instantaneous rate of change of software quality can be termed as instantaneous variation or simply variation. Now let us calculate the instantaneous variation at a particular stage, say time = 5 units. This can be done by calculating the average variation over different time periods and gradually reducing the time intervals in such a way that it nearly becomes zero at the stage of time = 5 units. See Figure 3.

It can be easily seen in the Figure 3 that the time interval is gradually being reduced towards the point at which we are going to calculate the instantaneous variation. At each interval, the slope of the line joining the two points on the curve gives the average variation in that interval. In the above Figure 3, the slopes of corresponding lines give the average variation between P_1Q_1 and P_2Q_2 respectively. Now, as the time interval becomes vanishingly small at the stage where time = 5 units, the secant becomes a tangent and then the average variation at that point becomes the slope of the tangent at that point of the curve. This average variation given by the slope of the tangent at that point is the instantaneous variation at that particular stage of software development. See Figure 4.

This means the calculation of instantaneous variation at any particular stage of software development is simply the calculation of the slope of the tangent to the quality versus development time curve at that particular stage.

Figure 3. Quality vs. time

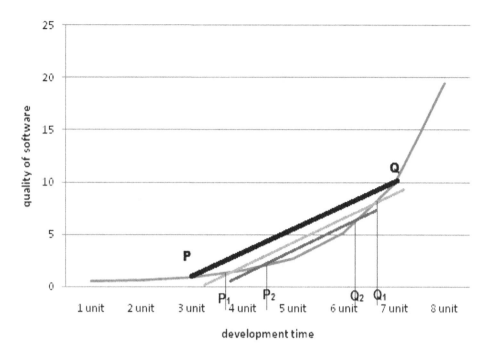

graph of quality versus time

From differential calculus, I know that the slope of any tangent to a curve at a particular point is given by the first derivative of the function representing the curve at that particular point. Thus, we can state the following expression for the instantaneous variation or simple variation:

$$[variation]_x = \left[\frac{dq}{dt}\right]_{t=x} \tag{5}$$

where $[variation]_x$ stands for variation at x.

As mentioned earlier, the quality can always be expressed as a function of development time. The function may vary from software to software and even from one organization to another. Each organization will be having its own set of attributes and methods to ascertain the relationship between the quality and the development time of the software. However, once this relation between the development time and quality is established, I can go forward to

Figure 4. Quality vs. time

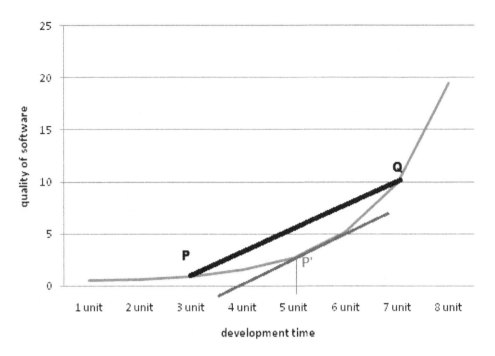

graph of quality versus time

simply finding the derivative at a particular point in time to get the expected instantaneous variation at that particular stage.

Likewise, I can also calculate the instantaneous variation with respect to the LOC. Only in this case I have to express quality as a function of the LOC. The figure 5is quality versus LOC has LOC count on the horizontal axis. The tangent to the curve at a particular value of LOC count gives the corresponding variation. The Figure 5 illustrates the point.

Figure 5 has shown quality vs. LOC with the help of Table 2.

I can see in the next figure that PQ will give us the average variation between the intervals of LOC = 500 to LOC = 3500. The slope of the tangent at P' will give the instantaneous variation when the LOC is exactly 2000. See Figure 6

I can calculate the variation with respect to the LOC in the same manner using differential calculus as I had done in the case of calculating variation with respect to development time. We get the expression as follows:

Table 2. Synthetic datasets (quality vs. LOC)

LOC	Quality
500	0.5
1000	13.3
1500	19.7
2000	22.9
2500	24.5
3000	25.3
3500	25.7
4000	25.9

Figure 5. Quality vs. LOC

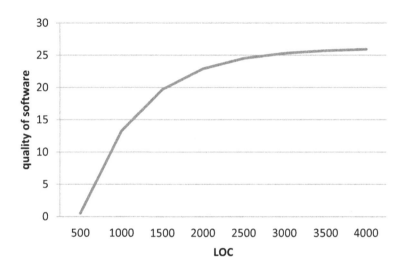

graph of quality versus LOC

$$\left[variation\right]_x = \left[\frac{dq}{dL}\right]_{L=x} \tag{6}$$

where

q = quality (to be expressed as a function of LOC).
L = normalized LOC.
$\left[variation\right]_x$ = instantaneous variation when LOC = x

Figure 6. Quality vs. LOC

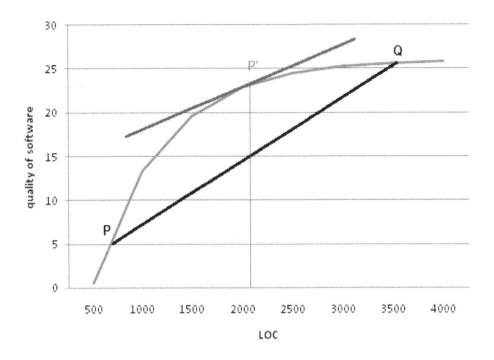

graph of quality versus LOC

$$\left[\frac{dq}{dL}\right]_{L=x} = \text{first derivative of the function quality w.r.t. LOC at the point where}$$
$$\text{LOC} = x$$

The calculation of variation has deep significance. It needs to be stressed at this juncture that the term variation used here is actually the variation of quality. Using the method shown here, I can calculate this variation in both space and time dimensions. When I am dealing with LOC, I am actually confronted with the size of the software. Then the calculation of variation deals with space dimensions.

Similarly, when I am dealing with development time, I am concerned with understanding the variation of quality in the time dimension. The concept of variation of quality in both space and time for the software gives a proper scientific metric that can be understood concretely and compared to accepted standards. Figure 7 is the model for calculation of variation.

Figure 7. Calculation of variation

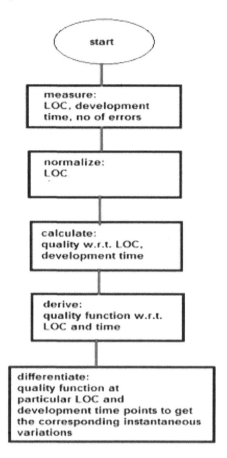

ACCELERATED AND RETARDED VARIATIONS

The variation as calculated in the above manner may be uniform, accelerated or retarded. First an overview of these terms is given as under:

1. **Uniform Variation:** When the change of quality of software remains the same over equal intervals of development time or over equal increase in LOC, the variation can be said to be uniform. If the software quality variation is uniform, there exists a linear relationship between the quality and development time or between the quality and the LOC. The graph drawn will invariably be a straight line as shown under. See Figure 8.

Figure 8 has shown quality vs. LOC with the help of Table 3.

Table 3. Synthetic datasets (quality vs. LOC)

LOC	Quality
500	0.5
1000	2.5
1500	4.5
2000	6.5
2500	8.5
3000	10.5
3500	12.5
4000	14.5

The same kind of figure can be seen if the horizontal component is development time. One can easily see that the ratio between the quality and the LOC or the development time, as the case is always remains a constant.

2. **Accelerated Variation:** When the increase in quality increases over equal intervals of time, I may call the situation a case of accelerated variation. The graph of an accelerated variation will be an overall concave curve with the slope of the curve, increasing over increase in LOC or

Figure 8. Synthetic datasets (uniform variation)

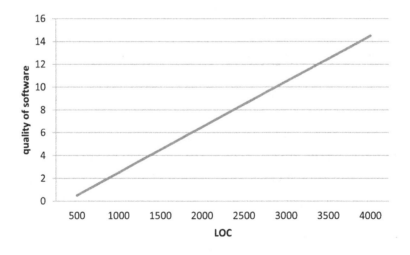

graph of quality versus LOC showing uniform variation

development time. The graph for an accelerated variation would look something like this. See Figure 9 (graph is based on Table 1).

It can be easily seen that the variation between the two stages P and Q and the variation between the two stages Q and R is not the same. The quality changes at different rates between P and Q and between different rates between Q and R. And it can also be easily seen that the variation is greater between Q and R than between P and Q. Thus, such a condition when the variation increases with successive stages of LOC growth or equal intervals of development time are called accelerated variation. The curve for an accelerated variation is a concave curve as shown in the Figure 9. Thus, if the graph of quality versus LOC or quality versus development time is a concave curve, we may conclude that on the whole it is an accelerated variation.

3. **Retarded Variation:** When the variation over successive equal intervals of development time or over successive stages of LOC growth goes on

Figure 9. Synthetic datasets (quality vs. time showing accelerated variation)

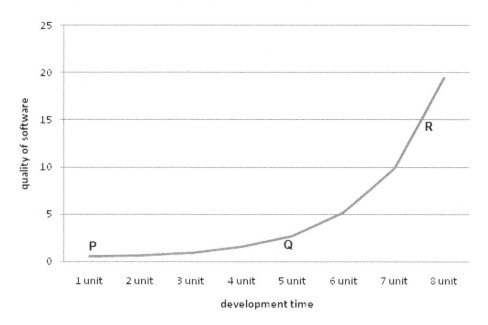

graph of quality versus time showing accelerated variation

diminishing we get the case of a retarded variation. The graph showing a retarded variation will be a convex with a mountain in it as shown in the Figure 10 (graph is based on Table 2).

Again, it is obvious that the change of quality between P and Q is not the same as the change of quality between Q and R. I can deduce that the variation is greater from P to Q that the variation between Q and R. If I compare this case with the earlier case, the difference is quite clear. In the earlier figure, the slope between P and Q is less than the slope between Q and R. While in this figure, the slope between P and Q is greater that the slope between Q and R. The rate of change of quality becomes slower in this case. Thus, I say that the average variation on the whole is gradually decreasing as through the life cycle of the software. This is a case of retarded variation. It is obvious from the above figure that on an average the figure of a retarded variation shows a convex curve. Thus, if the figure of quality versus LOC or the figure of quality versus development time is a convex curve, I can easily conclude that the variation is a retarded variation.

Figure 10. Synthetic datasets (quality vs. LOC showing retarded variation)

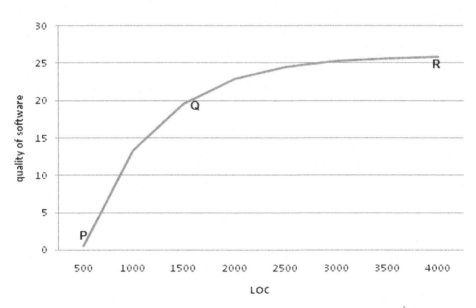

graph of quality versus LOC showing retarded variation

However, the average nature of variation is not as significant as the instantaneous nature of the variations. This is because at a particular stage of software development, the developer may be interested in finding out whether the change in software quality at that particular stage is going according to the set plan or not. For this it is necessary to determine whether the variation at any particular instance of development time or at any particular instance of code development is accelerated or retarded or uniform. As I have seen earlier that the curve for an accelerated variation is a concave curve and the curve for a retarded variation is a convex curve. So, if we just test the curvature of the graph at any particular instance of time, I shall be able to determine what the nature of variation is at that particular instance. Testing the curvature can be done according to the principles of differential calculus where I find the second derivative of the quality function with respect to the LOC or the development time as the case is. Now from differential calculus, if the second derivative at a particular point is positive, we have a concave curve at that point. Simultaneously, if the second derivative at a point is negative, I have a convex curve at that point. Mathematically stating I have the following:

If $\frac{d^2q}{dt^2} < 0$ or if $\frac{d^2q}{dL^2} < 0$ at $t = c$ or $L = c$ respectively, then at the particular stage c of software development, the variation curve is convex, showing a retardation in the variation. In the same way, if $\frac{d^2q}{dt^2} > 0$ or if $\frac{d^2q}{dL^2} > 0$ at $t = c$ or $L = c$ respectively, then at the particular stage c of software development, the variation curve is concave, showing an acceleration in the variation. There is another method of determining whether the variation at any particular stage of software development is accelerated or retarded. That is by using the method of increasing and decreasing functions. If at any particular point the figure of quality versus LOC or the figure of quality versus development time gives the indication of an increasing function, I can say that at that particular stage, there is accelerated variation. At the same time if at any particular stage of software development, the figure gives the indication of a decreasing function, I can conclude that at that particular stage of software development, the variation is retarded. I can decide whether the function is increasing or decreasing at any particular point by using the first derivative test. For this at a particular point first, we find the instantaneous variation. Then I determine the variation for a point just below and just above the point in consideration. If the value of the first derivative just below the consideration point is less than the first derivative at the consideration point and the first derivative at a point above the consideration point is just greater than the value of the first derivative at the considered point, then the conclusion will be that the function is increasing as it is passing through the considered point. On the contrary, if the first derivative at a point below is greater than the first derivative at the considered point and the first derivative at a point above is just greater than the first derivative at the point of consideration, I may conclude that the function is a decreasing function and thus it will follow that at that particular stage of software development, the variation is retarded.

A better understanding of the entire concept can be achieved from Figure 11.

As can be seen from the above figure that the slope of the tangent at Q (the stage where I wish to determine the nature of variation) has a variation greater than that at A but less than that at B. Hence this is a case of accelerated variation at Q. Similarly, see Figure 12.

It can be seen that the first derivative at Q is less than the first derivative at A but is greater than the first derivative at B. This is very obvious from the slopes of the tangents drawn at those particular points. This point towards

Figure 11. Synthetic datasets (quality vs. time showing accelerated variation)

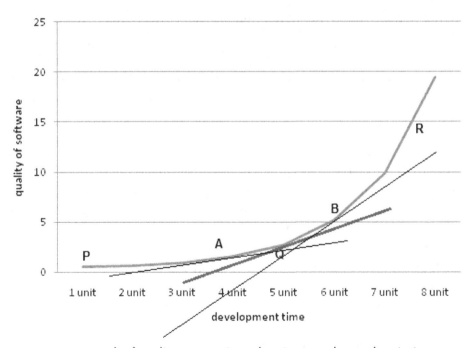

graph of quality versus time showing accelerated variation

Figure 12. Synthetic datasets (quality vs. LOC showing that variation is retarded at Q)

graph of quality versus LOC showing that variation is retarded at Q

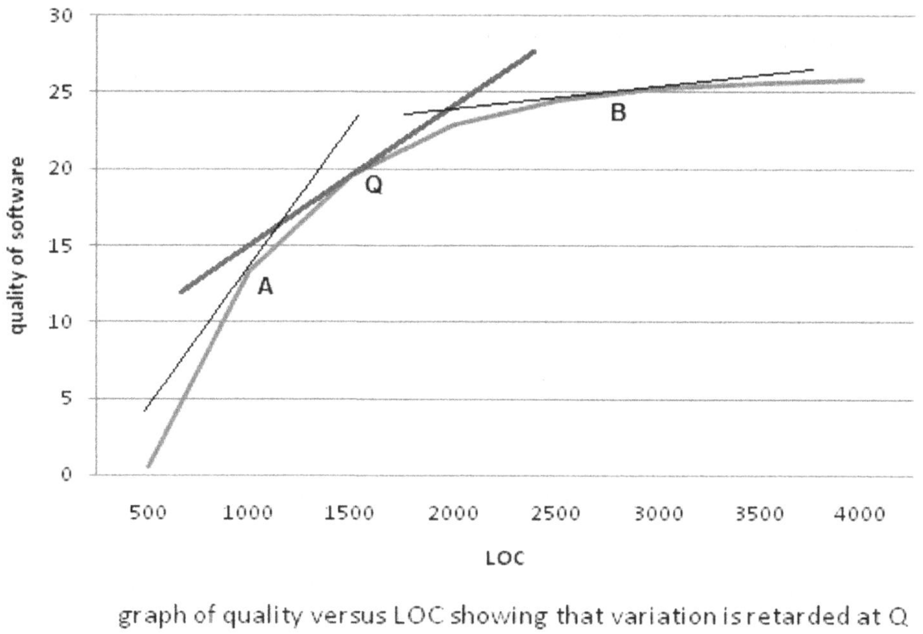

the fact that the function of quality with respect to the LOC is decreasing at the particular point Q. Thus I can conclude from this case that the software is undergoing a retarded variation at Q.

CONCLUSION

The chapter has presented a new method of estimating and evaluating the changes in quality through particular stages of software development. By measuring the changes in software development one can understand if the software development process is going through the expected phases. At the same time, I can estimate the probable quality of the final software. The estimation of changes in quality helps us to properly measure, compare and take concrete decisions regarding quality during the course of software development. The evaluation of the changes in quality gives the developer's ability to forecast the next stage or make adequate plans for the next phase of development. The method is mathematically motivated and its standards can be set up either by an international body or by any organization as per the requirement. This is not only a development in the realm of software development, but also adds to the treasure in the realm of applied mathematics. The use of graphical methods and other principles of differential calculus are clear pointers in that direction. There may be dispute about the method in which the various parameters are being calculated. Through repeated discussions and exchanges among experts, better methods of measurement of different parameters may evolve. Still, the method to decide the variation and the nature of variation will remain as enunciated in this chapter. Last but not the least; the chapter brings forward new ideas to be explored in the future. They may usher in a new arena of discussion altogether.

REFERENCES

Boehm, B. W. (1981). *Software Engineering Economics*. Upper Saddle River, NJ: Prentice Hall.

Conte, S. D., Dunsmore, H. E., & Shen, V. Y. (1986). *Software Engineering Metrics and Models*. Redwood City, CA: Benjamin-Cummins Publishing Co., Inc.

IEEE/American National Standards Institute (ANSI) standard (982.2). (n.d.). IEEE.

Kan, S. H. (2002). Metrics and Models in Software Quality Engineering (2nd ed.). New Delhi, India: Pearson Education.

Rashid, E., Patnaik, S., & Bhattacherjee, V. (2013). Estimation and evaluation of change in software quality at a particular stage of software development. *Indian Journal of Science and Technology*, 6(10).

Rashid, E., Patnaik, S., & Bhattacherjee, V. (2014). Prediction of rate of Improvement of Software Quality and Development Effort on the Basis of Degree of Excellence with respect to Number of Lines of Code. *International Journal of Computer Engineering and Applications, 5*(3), 6-13.

Conclusion

What I can conclude from the studies in this book is that a machine learning technique such as case-based reasoning can be applied for software quality predictions. The work carried out in the book is divided into nine chapters. Chapter 1 discusses the software quality. Chapter 2 enlightens the existing work to predict the quality of the software using various machine learning techniques. It also discussed scope of the present work.

The CBR model is easy to know mainly because it emulates an approach people use when faced with problem-solving situations in their everyday lives. When a person is faced with a new problem the first approach is generally to think about previous similar problems and to try to use the solutions to those problems, possibly with some changes, to solve the new problem. CBR solves problems in precisely this way by relying on specific knowledge about previous problems and their solutions. CBR systems often use indexing to partition the case base and cases to provide the specialized problem-solving knowledge. This is in addition to the application of different machine learning techniques for software quality estimation system properties (as investigated in Chapter 3).

There were also more specific conclusions, which can be drawn from this book, are given below:

1. The presented "Methods of software quality prediction with similarity measures: As an expert system" (as investigated in Chapter 4). The chapter tries to explore the importance of software fault prediction and to minimize them thoroughly with the advance knowledge of the error-prone modules, so as to enhance the software quality.
2. The computation of rate of improvement of quality and effort in the software development may add new dimensions to the understanding of software engineering. This chapter presented to develop a system to predict rate of improvement of the software quality at a particular point of

time with respect to the number of lines of code present in the software. In addition, the presented "quality estimation models" in software engineering are measured as degree of excellence (as investigated in Chapter 5).

3. The proposed new mathematical model is used to Measure the quality of software on the basis of time gap, quality gap and difference with standard model (as investigated in Chapter 6). This chapter suggests methods to calculate the difference in quality of the software being developed and the model software which has been decided upon as the criteria for comparison.

4. Chapter 7 presents some new ideas about estimation and evaluation of the quality of software. At the outset, it deals with the possibilities of using a standard conversion method so that lines of code from any language may be compared and be used as a uniform metric. This chapter also attempts to explain in depth the method of evaluating and understanding quality with respect to development time as well as LOC. Some new terms like efficiency and variation have been introduced to understand the change in software quality. The main focus is to evaluate and estimate software quality at a particular stage of software development. This is not average quality understanding, but quality estimation at a particular instance. The developer can evaluate the work at any stage using the methods given to review the present status and make future plans to meet the required target (as investigated in Chapter 7).

In this book, several models have been presented to predict software quality. Through empirical investigations and literature reviews conducted as part of this book, I anticipate a promising future where there are further research opportunities for evaluating the application of case-based reasoning in software quality prediction and software testing. The long-term goal of the research is as follows:

1. Increasing the volume of knowledgebase is another objective. The larger the database the more likely the results are to be accurate.

2. Use of neural network and/or fuzzy logic model for software quality prediction.

3. Addition of new parameters: Additional fields can be added to the record set so as to incorporate the dependency of the prediction if any, on these parameters. Till now, only those parameters were considered that had more dependency.

4. Addition of new similarity measures: Apart from Euclidean, Canberra, Exponential, Clark, and Manhattan methods other similarity measures can be used to find similar cases. For example, see the Chebychev method. Choice in the use of similarity measure adds flexibility to the system and allows to compare among the methods.

5. The method of predicting the quality of the final software is a part of the future work.

6. The significance of the ratio between the quality gap and time gap are areas for future work. They need to be studied and hypnotized separately as a separate piece of research work.

Glossary

CBR: Case-Based Reasoning.

DL: Difficulty level.

DT: Development Time.

FS: Fuzzy System.

KB: General Knowledge.

KBS: Knowledgebase.

MLR: Multiple Linear Regression.

MRE: Magnitude of Relative Error.

NFUNC: Number of functions.

NLOC: Number of lines of code.

NLOC+NFUNC: Number of lines of code + Number of functions.

NN: Neural Networks.

PEX: Programmers experience.

RBS: Rule-Based Systems.

RT: Regression Tree.

WCD: Weighted Canberra distance.

WC$_L$D: Weighted Clark distance.

WED: Weighted Euclidean distance.

WE$_X$D: Weighted Exponential distance.

WMD: Weighted Manhattan distance.

Related Readings

To continue IGI Global's long-standing tradition of advancing innovation through emerging research, please find below a compiled list of recommended IGI Global book chapters and journal articles in the areas of human-computer interaction, artificial intelligence, and smart environments. These related readings will provide additional information and guidance to further enrich your knowledge and assist you with your own research.

Abdulrahman, M. D., Subramanian, N., Chan, H. K., & Ning, K. (2017). Big Data Analytics: Academic Perspectives. In H. Chan, N. Subramanian, & M. Abdulrahman (Eds.), *Supply Chain Management in the Big Data Era* (pp. 1–12). Hershey, PA: IGI Global. doi:10.4018/978-1-5225-0956-1.ch001

Al-Aiad, A., Alkhatib, K., Al-Ayyad, M., & Hmeidi, I. (2016). A Conceptual Framework of Smart Home Context: An Empirical Investigation. *International Journal of Healthcare Information Systems and Informatics*, *11*(3), 42–56. doi:10.4018/IJHISI.2016070103

Almajano, P., Lopez-Sanchez, M., Rodriguez, I., Puig, A., Llorente, M. S., & Ribera, M. (2016). Training Infrastructure to Participate in Real Life Institutions: Learning through Virtual Worlds. In F. Neto, R. de Souza, & A. Gomes (Eds.), *Handbook of Research on 3-D Virtual Environments and Hypermedia for Ubiquitous Learning* (pp. 192–219). Hershey, PA: IGI Global. doi:10.4018/978-1-5225-0125-1.ch008

Ammari, H. M., Shaout, A., & Mustapha, F. (2017). Sensing Coverage in Three-Dimensional Space: A Survey. In N. Ray & A. Turuk (Eds.), *Handbook of Research on Advanced Wireless Sensor Network Applications, Protocols, and Architectures* (pp. 1–28). Hershey, PA: IGI Global. doi:10.4018/978-1-5225-0486-3.ch001

Ang, L., Seng, K. P., & Heng, T. Z. (2016). Information Communication Assistive Technologies for Visually Impaired People. *International Journal of Ambient Computing and Intelligence*, 7(1), 45–68. doi:10.4018/IJACI.2016010103

Ang, R. P., Tan, J. L., Goh, D. H., Huan, V. S., Ooi, Y. P., Boon, J. S., & Fung, D. S. (2017). A Game-Based Approach to Teaching Social Problem-Solving Skills. In R. Zheng & M. Gardner (Eds.), *Handbook of Research on Serious Games for Educational Applications* (pp. 168–195). Hershey, PA: IGI Global. doi:10.4018/978-1-5225-0513-6.ch008

Anthopoulos, L., Janssen, M., & Weerakkody, V. (2016). A Unified Smart City Model (USCM) for Smart City Conceptualization and Benchmarking. *International Journal of Electronic Government Research*, 12(2), 77–93. doi:10.4018/IJEGR.2016040105

Antonova, A. (2017). Preparing for the Forthcoming Industrial Revolution: Beyond Virtual Worlds Technologies for Competence Development and Learning. *International Journal of Virtual and Augmented Reality*, 1(1), 16–28. doi:10.4018/IJVAR.2017010102

Applin, S. A., & Fischer, M. D. (2017). Thing Theory: Connecting Humans to Smart Healthcare. In C. Reis & M. Maximiano (Eds.), *Internet of Things and Advanced Application in Healthcare* (pp. 249–265). Hershey, PA: IGI Global. doi:10.4018/978-1-5225-1820-4.ch009

Armstrong, S., & Yampolskiy, R. V. (2017). Security Solutions for Intelligent and Complex Systems. In M. Dawson, M. Eltayeb, & M. Omar (Eds.), *Security Solutions for Hyperconnectivity and the Internet of Things* (pp. 37–88). Hershey, PA: IGI Global. doi:10.4018/978-1-5225-0741-3.ch003

Auza, J. M., & de Marca, J. R. (2017). A Mobility Model for Crowd Sensing Simulation. *International Journal of Interdisciplinary Telecommunications and Networking*, 9(1), 14–25. doi:10.4018/IJITN.2017010102

Ayesh, A., Arevalillo-Herráez, M., & Ferri, F. J. (2016). Towards Psychologically based Personalised Modelling of Emotions Using Associative Classifiers. *International Journal of Cognitive Informatics and Natural Intelligence*, *10*(2), 52–64. doi:10.4018/IJCINI.2016040103

Badilla, G. L., & Gaynor, J. M. (2017). Analysis of New Opotoelectronic Device for Detection of Heavy Metals in Corroded Soils: Design a Novel Optoelectronic Devices. In O. Sergiyenko & J. Rodriguez-Quiñonez (Eds.), *Developing and Applying Optoelectronics in Machine Vision* (pp. 273–302). Hershey, PA: IGI Global. doi:10.4018/978-1-5225-0632-4.ch009

Balas, C. E. (2016). An Artificial Neural Network Model as the Decision Support System of Ports. In E. Ocalir-Akunal (Ed.), *Using Decision Support Systems for Transportation Planning Efficiency* (pp. 36–60). Hershey, PA: IGI Global. doi:10.4018/978-1-4666-8648-9.ch002

Barbeito, A., Painho, M., Cabral, P., & ONeill, J. G. (2017). Beyond Digital Human Body Atlases: Segmenting an Integrated 3D Topological Model of the Human Body. *International Journal of E-Health and Medical Communications*, *8*(1), 19–36. doi:10.4018/IJEHMC.2017010102

Berrahal, S., & Boudriga, N. (2017). The Risks of Wearable Technologies to Individuals and Organizations. In A. Marrington, D. Kerr, & J. Gammack (Eds.), *Managing Security Issues and the Hidden Dangers of Wearable Technologies* (pp. 18–46). Hershey, PA: IGI Global. doi:10.4018/978-1-5225-1016-1.ch002

Bhargavi, P., Jyothi, S., & Mamatha, D. M. (2017). A Study on Hybridization of Intelligent Techniques in Bioinformatics. In S. Bhattacharyya, S. De, I. Pan, & P. Dutta (Eds.), *Intelligent Multidimensional Data Clustering and Analysis* (pp. 358–379). Hershey, PA: IGI Global. doi:10.4018/978-1-5225-1776-4.ch014

Bhattacharya, S. (2017). A Predictive Linear Regression Model for Affective State Detection of Mobile Touch Screen Users. *International Journal of Mobile Human Computer Interaction*, *9*(1), 30–44. doi:10.4018/IJMHCI.2017010103

Biagi, L., Comai, S., Mangiarotti, R., Matteucci, M., Negretti, M., & Yavuz, S. U. (2017). Enriching Geographic Maps with Accessible Paths Derived from Implicit Mobile Device Data Collection. In S. Konomi & G. Roussos (Eds.), *Enriching Urban Spaces with Ambient Computing, the Internet of Things, and Smart City Design* (pp. 89–113). Hershey, PA: IGI Global. doi:10.4018/978-1-5225-0827-4.ch005

Bogatinov, D. S., Bogdanoski, M., & Angelevski, S. (2016). AI-Based Cyber Defense for More Secure Cyberspace. In M. Hadji-Janev & M. Bogdanoski (Eds.), *Handbook of Research on Civil Society and National Security in the Era of Cyber Warfare* (pp. 220–237). Hershey, PA: IGI Global. doi:10.4018/978-1-4666-8793-6.ch011

Bottrighi, A., Leonardi, G., Piovesan, L., & Terenziani, P. (2016). Knowledge-Based Support to the Treatment of Exceptions in Computer Interpretable Clinical Guidelines. *International Journal of Knowledge-Based Organizations*, *6*(3), 1–27. doi:10.4018/IJKBO.2016070101

Bureš, V., Tučník, P., Mikulecký, P., Mls, K., & Blecha, P. (2016). Application of Ambient Intelligence in Educational Institutions: Visions and Architectures. *International Journal of Ambient Computing and Intelligence*, *7*(1), 94–120. doi:10.4018/IJACI.2016010105

Castellet, A. (2016). What If Devices Take Command: Content Innovation Perspectives for Smart Wearables in the Mobile Ecosystem. *International Journal of Handheld Computing Research*, *7*(2), 16–33. doi:10.4018/IJHCR.2016040102

Champaty, B., Ray, S. S., Mohapatra, B., & Pal, K. (2017). Voluntary Blink Controlled Communication Protocol for Bed-Ridden Patients. In N. Kamila (Ed.), *Handbook of Research on Wireless Sensor Network Trends, Technologies, and Applications* (pp. 162–195). Hershey, PA: IGI Global. doi:10.4018/978-1-5225-0501-3.ch008

Chawla, S. (2017). Multi-Agent-Based Information Retrieval System Using Information Scent in Query Log Mining for Effective Web Search. In G. Sreedhar (Ed.), *Web Data Mining and the Development of Knowledge-Based Decision Support Systems* (pp. 131–156). Hershey, PA: IGI Global. doi:10.4018/978-1-5225-1877-8.ch008

Chen, G., Wang, E., Sun, X., & Lu, Y. (2016). An Intelligent Approval System for City Construction based on Cloud Computing and Big Data. *International Journal of Grid and High Performance Computing*, *8*(3), 57–69. doi:10.4018/IJGHPC.2016070104

Cointault, F., Han, S., Rabatel, G., Jay, S., Rousseau, D., Billiot, B., & Salon, C. et al. (2017). 3D Imaging Systems for Agricultural Applications: Characterization of Crop and Root Phenotyping. In O. Sergiyenko & J. Rodriguez-Quiñonez (Eds.), *Developing and Applying Optoelectronics in Machine Vision* (pp. 236–272). Hershey, PA: IGI Global. doi:10.4018/978-1-5225-0632-4.ch008

Connor, A. M. (2016). A Historical Review of Creative Technologies. In A. Connor & S. Marks (Eds.), *Creative Technologies for Multidisciplinary Applications* (pp. 1–24). Hershey, PA: IGI Global. doi:10.4018/978-1-5225-0016-2.ch001

Connor, A. M., Sosa, R., Karmokar, S., Marks, S., Buxton, M., Gribble, A. M., & Foottit, J. et al. (2016). Exposing Core Competencies for Future Creative Technologists. In A. Connor & S. Marks (Eds.), *Creative Technologies for Multidisciplinary Applications* (pp. 377–397). Hershey, PA: IGI Global. doi:10.4018/978-1-5225-0016-2.ch015

Cook, A. E., & Wei, W. (2017). Using Eye Movements to Study Reading Processes: Methodological Considerations. In C. Was, F. Sansosti, & B. Morris (Eds.), *Eye-Tracking Technology Applications in Educational Research* (pp. 27–47). Hershey, PA: IGI Global. doi:10.4018/978-1-5225-1005-5.ch002

Corradini, A., & Mehta, M. (2016). A Graphical Tool for the Creation of Behaviors in Virtual Worlds. In J. Turner, M. Nixon, U. Bernardet, & S. DiPaola (Eds.), *Integrating Cognitive Architectures into Virtual Character Design* (pp. 65–93). Hershey, PA: IGI Global. doi:10.4018/978-1-5225-0454-2.ch003

Corrêa, L. D., & Dorn, M. (2017). Multi-Agent Systems in Three-Dimensional Protein Structure Prediction. In D. Adamatti (Ed.), *Multi-Agent-Based Simulations Applied to Biological and Environmental Systems* (pp. 241–278). Hershey, PA: IGI Global. doi:10.4018/978-1-5225-1756-6.ch011

Croatti, A., Ricci, A., & Viroli, M. (2017). Towards a Mobile Augmented Reality System for Emergency Management: The Case of SAFE. *International Journal of Distributed Systems and Technologies*, 8(1), 46–58. doi:10.4018/IJDST.2017010104

Dafer, M., & El-Abed, M. (2017). Evaluation of Keystroke Dynamics Authentication Systems: Analysis of Physical and Touch Screen Keyboards. In M. Dawson, D. Kisku, P. Gupta, J. Sing, & W. Li (Eds.), *Developing Next-Generation Countermeasures for Homeland Security Threat Prevention* (pp. 306–329). Hershey, PA: IGI Global. doi:10.4018/978-1-5225-0703-1.ch014

Das, P. K., Ghosh, D., Jagtap, P., Joshi, A., & Finin, T. (2017). Preserving User Privacy and Security in Context-Aware Mobile Platforms. In S. Mukherjea (Ed.), *Mobile Application Development, Usability, and Security* (pp. 166–193). Hershey, PA: IGI Global. doi:10.4018/978-1-5225-0945-5.ch008

De Filippi, F., Coscia, C., & Guido, R. (2017). How Technologies Can Enhance Open Policy Making and Citizen-Responsive Urban Planning: MiraMap - A Governing Tool for the Mirafiori Sud District in Turin (Italy). *International Journal of E-Planning Research, 6*(1), 23–42. doi:10.4018/IJEPR.2017010102

De Pasquale, D., Wood, E., Gottardo, A., Jones, J. A., Kaplan, R., & DeMarco, A. (2017). Tracking Children's Interactions with Traditional Text and Computer-Based Early Literacy Media. In C. Was, F. Sansosti, & B. Morris (Eds.), *Eye-Tracking Technology Applications in Educational Research* (pp. 107–121). Hershey, PA: IGI Global. doi:10.4018/978-1-5225-1005-5.ch006

Del Fiore, G., Mainetti, L., Mighali, V., Patrono, L., Alletto, S., Cucchiara, R., & Serra, G. (2016). A Location-Aware Architecture for an IoT-Based Smart Museum. *International Journal of Electronic Government Research, 12*(2), 39–55. doi:10.4018/IJEGR.2016040103

Desjarlais, M. (2017). The Use of Eye-gaze to Understand Multimedia Learning. In C. Was, F. Sansosti, & B. Morris (Eds.), *Eye-Tracking Technology Applications in Educational Research* (pp. 122–142). Hershey, PA: IGI Global. doi:10.4018/978-1-5225-1005-5.ch007

Diviacco, P., & Leadbetter, A. (2017). Balancing Formalization and Representation in Cross-Domain Data Management for Sustainable Development. In P. Diviacco, A. Leadbetter, & H. Glaves (Eds.), *Oceanographic and Marine Cross-Domain Data Management for Sustainable Development* (pp. 23–46). Hershey, PA: IGI Global. doi:10.4018/978-1-5225-0700-0.ch002

Dragoicea, M., Falcao e Cunha, J., Alexandru, M. V., & Constantinescu, D. A. (2017). Modelling and Simulation Perspective in Service Design: Experience in Transport Information Service Development. In S. Rozenes & Y. Cohen (Eds.), *Handbook of Research on Strategic Alliances and Value Co-Creation in the Service Industry* (pp. 374–399). Hershey, PA: IGI Global. doi:10.4018/978-1-5225-2084-9.ch019

El Khayat, G. A., & Fashal, N. A. (2017). Inter and Intra Cities Smartness: A Survey on Location Problems and GIS Tools. In S. Faiz & K. Mahmoudi (Eds.), *Handbook of Research on Geographic Information Systems Applications and Advancements* (pp. 296–320). Hershey, PA: IGI Global. doi:10.4018/978-1-5225-0937-0.ch011

Eteme, A. A., & Ngossaha, J. M. (2017). Urban Master Data Management: Case of the YUSIIP Platform. In S. Faiz & K. Mahmoudi (Eds.), *Handbook of Research on Geographic Information Systems Applications and Advancements* (pp. 441–465). Hershey, PA: IGI Global. doi:10.4018/978-1-5225-0937-0.ch018

Fisher, K. J., Nichols, T., Isbister, K., & Fuller, T. (2017). Quantifying "Magic": Creating Good Player Experiences on Xbox Kinect. In B. Dubbels (Ed.), *Transforming Gaming and Computer Simulation Technologies across Industries* (pp. 1–16). Hershey, PA: IGI Global. doi:10.4018/978-1-5225-1817-4.ch001

Flores-Fuentes, W., Rivas-Lopez, M., Hernandez-Balbuena, D., Sergiyenko, O., Rodríguez-Quiñonez, J. C., Rivera-Castillo, J., & Basaca-Preciado, L. C. et al. (2017). Applying Optoelectronic Devices Fusion in Machine Vision: Spatial Coordinate Measurement. In O. Sergiyenko & J. Rodriguez-Quiñonez (Eds.), *Developing and Applying Optoelectronics in Machine Vision* (pp. 1–37). Hershey, PA: IGI Global. doi:10.4018/978-1-5225-0632-4.ch001

Forti, I. (2017). A Cross Reading of Landscape through Digital Landscape Models: The Case of Southern Garda. In A. Ippolito (Ed.), *Handbook of Research on Emerging Technologies for Architectural and Archaeological Heritage* (pp. 532–561). Hershey, PA: IGI Global. doi:10.4018/978-1-5225-0675-1.ch018

Gammack, J., & Marrington, A. (2017). The Promise and Perils of Wearable Technologies. In A. Marrington, D. Kerr, & J. Gammack (Eds.), *Managing Security Issues and the Hidden Dangers of Wearable Technologies* (pp. 1–17). Hershey, PA: IGI Global. doi:10.4018/978-1-5225-1016-1.ch001

Ghaffarianhoseini, A., Ghaffarianhoseini, A., Tookey, J., Omrany, H., Fleury, A., Naismith, N., & Ghaffarianhoseini, M. (2016). The Essence of Smart Homes: Application of Intelligent Technologies towards Smarter Urban Future. In A. Connor & S. Marks (Eds.), *Creative Technologies for Multidisciplinary Applications* (pp. 334–376). Hershey, PA: IGI Global. doi:10.4018/978-1-5225-0016-2.ch014

Gharbi, A., De Runz, C., & Akdag, H. (2017). Urban Development Modelling: A Survey. In S. Faiz & K. Mahmoudi (Eds.), *Handbook of Research on Geographic Information Systems Applications and Advancements* (pp. 96–124). Hershey, PA: IGI Global. doi:10.4018/978-1-5225-0937-0.ch004

Ghosh, S., Mitra, S., Ghosh, S., & Chakraborty, S. (2017). Seismic Reliability Analysis in the Framework of Metamodelling Based Monte Carlo Simulation. In P. Samui, S. Chakraborty, & D. Kim (Eds.), *Modeling and Simulation Techniques in Structural Engineering* (pp. 192–208). Hershey, PA: IGI Global. doi:10.4018/978-1-5225-0588-4.ch006

Guesgen, H. W., & Marsland, S. (2016). Using Contextual Information for Recognising Human Behaviour. *International Journal of Ambient Computing and Intelligence*, 7(1), 27–44. doi:10.4018/IJACI.2016010102

Hameur Laine, A., & Brahimi, S. (2017). Background on Context-Aware Computing Systems. In C. Reis & M. Maximiano (Eds.), *Internet of Things and Advanced Application in Healthcare* (pp. 1–31). Hershey, PA: IGI Global. doi:10.4018/978-1-5225-1820-4.ch001

Harrati, N., Bouchrika, I., Mahfouf, Z., & Ladjailia, A. (2017). Evaluation Methods for E-Learning Applications in Terms of User Satisfaction and Interface Usability. In P. Vu, S. Fredrickson, & C. Moore (Eds.), *Handbook of Research on Innovative Pedagogies and Technologies for Online Learning in Higher Education* (pp. 427–448). Hershey, PA: IGI Global. doi:10.4018/978-1-5225-1851-8.ch018

Harwood, T. (2016). Machinima: A Meme of Our Time. In A. Connor & S. Marks (Eds.), *Creative Technologies for Multidisciplinary Applications* (pp. 149–181). Hershey, PA: IGI Global. doi:10.4018/978-1-5225-0016-2.ch007

Hassani, K., & Lee, W. (2016). A Universal Architecture for Migrating Cognitive Agents: A Case Study on Automatic Animation Generation. In J. Turner, M. Nixon, U. Bernardet, & S. DiPaola (Eds.), *Integrating Cognitive Architectures into Virtual Character Design* (pp. 238–265). Hershey, PA: IGI Global. doi:10.4018/978-1-5225-0454-2.ch009

Herpich, F., Nunes, F. B., Voss, G. B., & Medina, R. D. (2016). Three-Dimensional Virtual Environment and NPC: A Perspective about Intelligent Agents Ubiquitous. In F. Neto, R. de Souza, & A. Gomes (Eds.), *Handbook of Research on 3-D Virtual Environments and Hypermedia for Ubiquitous Learning* (pp. 510–536). Hershey, PA: IGI Global. doi:10.4018/978-1-5225-0125-1.ch021

Higgins, C., Kearns, Á., Ryan, C., & Fernstrom, M. (2016). The Role of Gamification and Evolutionary Computation in the Provision of Self-Guided Speech Therapy. In D. Novák, B. Tulu, & H. Brendryen (Eds.), *Handbook of Research on Holistic Perspectives in Gamification for Clinical Practice* (pp. 158–182). Hershey, PA: IGI Global. doi:10.4018/978-1-4666-9522-1.ch008

Honarvar, A. R., & Sami, A. (2016). Extracting Usage Patterns from Power Usage Data of Homes Appliances in Smart Home using Big Data Platform. *International Journal of Information Technology and Web Engineering*, *11*(2), 39–50. doi:10.4018/IJITWE.2016040103

Hulsey, N. (2016). Between Games and Simulation: Gamification and Convergence in Creative Computing. In A. Connor & S. Marks (Eds.), *Creative Technologies for Multidisciplinary Applications* (pp. 130–148). Hershey, PA: IGI Global. doi:10.4018/978-1-5225-0016-2.ch006

Ion, A., & Patrascu, M. (2017). Agent Based Modelling of Smart Structures: The Challenges of a New Research Domain. In P. Samui, S. Chakraborty, & D. Kim (Eds.), *Modeling and Simulation Techniques in Structural Engineering* (pp. 38–60). Hershey, PA: IGI Global. doi:10.4018/978-1-5225-0588-4.ch002

Iyawe, B. I. (2017). User Performance Testing Indicator: User Performance Indicator Tool (UPIT). In S. Saeed, Y. Bamarouf, T. Ramayah, & S. Iqbal (Eds.), *Design Solutions for User-Centric Information Systems* (pp. 205–229). Hershey, PA: IGI Global. doi:10.4018/978-1-5225-1944-7.ch012

Izumi, S., Hata, M., Takahira, H., Soylu, M., Edo, A., Abe, T., & Suganuma, T. (2017). A Proposal of SDN Based Disaster-Aware Smart Routing for Highly-Available Information Storage Systems and Its Evaluation. *International Journal of Software Science and Computational Intelligence*, *9*(1), 68–82. doi:10.4018/IJSSCI.2017010105

Jarušek, R., & Kocian, V. (2017). Artificial Intelligence Algorithms for Classification and Pattern Recognition. In E. Volna, M. Kotyrba, & M. Janosek (Eds.), *Pattern Recognition and Classification in Time Series Data* (pp. 53–85). Hershey, PA: IGI Global. doi:10.4018/978-1-5225-0565-5.ch003

Jayabalan, J., Yildirim, D., Kim, D., & Samui, P. (2017). Design Optimization of a Wind Turbine Using Artificial Intelligence. In M. Ram & J. Davim (Eds.), *Mathematical Concepts and Applications in Mechanical Engineering and Mechatronics* (pp. 38–66). Hershey, PA: IGI Global. doi:10.4018/978-1-5225-1639-2.ch003

Jena, G. C. (2017). Multi-Sensor Data Fusion (MSDF). In N. Ray & A. Turuk (Eds.), *Handbook of Research on Advanced Wireless Sensor Network Applications, Protocols, and Architectures* (pp. 29–61). Hershey, PA: IGI Global. doi:10.4018/978-1-5225-0486-3.ch002

Kale, G. V., & Patil, V. H. (2016). A Study of Vision based Human Motion Recognition and Analysis. *International Journal of Ambient Computing and Intelligence*, *7*(2), 75–92. doi:10.4018/IJACI.2016070104

Kasemsap, K. (2017). Mastering Intelligent Decision Support Systems in Enterprise Information Management. In G. Sreedhar (Ed.), *Web Data Mining and the Development of Knowledge-Based Decision Support Systems* (pp. 35–56). Hershey, PA: IGI Global. doi:10.4018/978-1-5225-1877-8.ch004

Kim, S. (2017). New Game Paradigm for IoT Systems. In *Game Theory Solutions for the Internet of Things: Emerging Research and Opportunities* (pp. 101–147). Hershey, PA: IGI Global. doi:10.4018/978-1-5225-1952-2.ch004

Ladjailia, A., Bouchrika, I., Harrati, N., & Mahfouf, Z. (2017). Encoding Human Motion for Automated Activity Recognition in Surveillance Applications. In N. Dey, A. Ashour, & S. Acharjee (Eds.), *Applied Video Processing in Surveillance and Monitoring Systems* (pp. 170–192). Hershey, PA: IGI Global. doi:10.4018/978-1-5225-1022-2.ch008

Lanza, J., Sotres, P., Sánchez, L., Galache, J. A., Santana, J. R., Gutiérrez, V., & Muñoz, L. (2016). Managing Large Amounts of Data Generated by a Smart City Internet of Things Deployment. *International Journal on Semantic Web and Information Systems*, *12*(4), 22–42. doi:10.4018/IJSWIS.2016100102

Lee, H. (2017). The Internet of Things and Assistive Technologies for People with Disabilities: Applications, Trends, and Issues. In C. Reis & M. Maximiano (Eds.), *Internet of Things and Advanced Application in Healthcare* (pp. 32–65). Hershey, PA: IGI Global. doi:10.4018/978-1-5225-1820-4.ch002

Li, W. H., Zhu, K., & Fu, H. (2017). Exploring the Design Space of Bezel-Initiated Gestures for Mobile Interaction. *International Journal of Mobile Human Computer Interaction*, *9*(1), 16–29. doi:10.4018/IJMHCI.2017010102

Ludwig, T., Kotthaus, C., & Pipek, V. (2015). Should I Try Turning It Off and On Again?: Outlining HCI Challenges for Cyber-Physical Production Systems. *International Journal of Information Systems for Crisis Response and Management*, *7*(3), 55–68. doi:10.4018/ijiscram.2015070104

Luo, L., Kiewra, K. A., Peteranetz, M. S., & Flanigan, A. E. (2017). Using Eye-Tracking Technology to Understand How Graphic Organizers Aid Student Learning. In C. Was, F. Sansosti, & B. Morris (Eds.), *Eye-Tracking Technology Applications in Educational Research* (pp. 220–238). Hershey, PA: IGI Global. doi:10.4018/978-1-5225-1005-5.ch011

Mahanty, R., & Mahanti, P. K. (2016). Unleashing Artificial Intelligence onto Big Data: A Review. In S. Dash & B. Subudhi (Eds.), *Handbook of Research on Computational Intelligence Applications in Bioinformatics* (pp. 1–16). Hershey, PA: IGI Global. doi:10.4018/978-1-5225-0427-6.ch001

Marzuki, A. (2017). CMOS Image Sensor: Analog and Mixed-Signal Circuits. In O. Sergiyenko & J. Rodriguez-Quiñonez (Eds.), *Developing and Applying Optoelectronics in Machine Vision* (pp. 38–78). Hershey, PA: IGI Global. doi:10.4018/978-1-5225-0632-4.ch002

McKenna, H. P. (2017). Urbanizing the Ambient: Why People Matter So Much in Smart Cities. In S. Konomi & G. Roussos (Eds.), *Enriching Urban Spaces with Ambient Computing, the Internet of Things, and Smart City Design* (pp. 209–231). Hershey, PA: IGI Global. doi:10.4018/978-1-5225-0827-4.ch011

Meghanathan, N. (2017). Diameter-Aggregation Delay Tradeoff for Data Gathering Trees in Wireless Sensor Networks. In N. Kamila (Ed.), *Handbook of Research on Wireless Sensor Network Trends, Technologies, and Applications* (pp. 237–253). Hershey, PA: IGI Global. doi:10.4018/978-1-5225-0501-3. ch010

Moein, S. (2014). Artificial Intelligence in Medical Science. In *Medical Diagnosis Using Artificial Neural Networks* (pp. 11–23). Hershey, PA: IGI Global. doi:10.4018/978-1-4666-6146-2.ch002

Moein, S. (2014). Artificial Neural Network for Medical Diagnosis. In *Medical Diagnosis Using Artificial Neural Networks* (pp. 85–94). Hershey, PA: IGI Global. doi:10.4018/978-1-4666-6146-2.ch007

Moein, S. (2014). Types of Artificial Neural Network. In *Medical Diagnosis Using Artificial Neural Networks* (pp. 58–67). Hershey, PA: IGI Global. doi:10.4018/978-1-4666-6146-2.ch005

Moser, S. (2017). Linking Virtual and Real-life Environments: Scrutinizing Ubiquitous Learning Scenarios. In S. Şad & M. Ebner (Eds.), *Digital Tools for Seamless Learning* (pp. 214–239). Hershey, PA: IGI Global. doi:10.4018/978-1-5225-1692-7.ch011

Mumini, O. O., Adebisi, F. M., Edward, O. O., & Abidemi, A. S. (2016). Simulation of Stock Prediction System using Artificial Neural Networks. *International Journal of Business Analytics*, *3*(3), 25–44. doi:10.4018/ IJBAN.2016070102

Muñoz, M. C., & Moh, M. (2017). Authentication of Smart Grid: The Case for Using Merkle Trees. In M. Ferrag & A. Ahmim (Eds.), *Security Solutions and Applied Cryptography in Smart Grid Communications* (pp. 117–136). Hershey, PA: IGI Global. doi:10.4018/978-1-5225-1829-7.ch007

Mushcab, H., Kernohan, W. G., Wallace, J., Harper, R., & Martin, S. (2017). Self-Management of Diabetes Mellitus with Remote Monitoring: A Retrospective Review of 214 Cases. *International Journal of E-Health and Medical Communications*, *8*(1), 52–61. doi:10.4018/IJEHMC.2017010104

Mutlu-Bayraktar, D. (2017). Usability Evaluation of Social Media Web Sites and Applications via Eye-Tracking Method. In S. Hai-Jew (Ed.), *Social Media Data Extraction and Content Analysis* (pp. 85–112). Hershey, PA: IGI Global. doi:10.4018/978-1-5225-0648-5.ch004

Nadler, S. (2017). Mobile Location Tracking: Indoor and Outdoor Location Tracking. In S. Mukherjea (Ed.), *Mobile Application Development, Usability, and Security* (pp. 194–209). Hershey, PA: IGI Global. doi:10.4018/978-1-5225-0945-5.ch009

Nagpal, R., Mehrotra, D., & Bhatia, P. K. (2017). The State of Art in Website Usability Evaluation Methods. In S. Saeed, Y. Bamarouf, T. Ramayah, & S. Iqbal (Eds.), *Design Solutions for User-Centric Information Systems* (pp. 275–296). Hershey, PA: IGI Global. doi:10.4018/978-1-5225-1944-7.ch015

Nava, J., & Osorio, A. (2016). A Hybrid Intelligent Risk Identification Model for Configuration Management in Aerospace Systems. In A. Ochoa-Zezzatti, J. Sánchez, M. Cedillo-Campos, & M. de Lourdes (Eds.), *Handbook of Research on Military, Aeronautical, and Maritime Logistics and Operations* (pp. 319–345). Hershey, PA: IGI Global. doi:10.4018/978-1-4666-9779-9.ch017

Nazareth, A., Odean, R., & Pruden, S. M. (2017). The Use of Eye-Tracking in Spatial Thinking Research. In C. Was, F. Sansosti, & B. Morris (Eds.), *Eye-Tracking Technology Applications in Educational Research* (pp. 239–260). Hershey, PA: IGI Global. doi:10.4018/978-1-5225-1005-5.ch012

Neves, J., Zeleznikow, J., & Vicente, H. (2016). Quality of Judgment Assessment. In P. Novais & D. Carneiro (Eds.), *Interdisciplinary Perspectives on Contemporary Conflict Resolution* (pp. 96–110). Hershey, PA: IGI Global. doi:10.4018/978-1-5225-0245-6.ch006

Niewiadomski, R., & Anderson, D. (2017). The Rise of Artificial Intelligence: Its Impact on Labor Market and Beyond. In R. Batko & A. Szopa (Eds.), *Strategic Imperatives and Core Competencies in the Era of Robotics and Artificial Intelligence* (pp. 29–49). Hershey, PA: IGI Global. doi:10.4018/978-1-5225-1656-9.ch003

Nishani, L., & Biba, M. (2017). Statistical Relational Learning for Collaborative Filtering a State-of-the-Art Review. In V. Bhatnagar (Ed.), *Collaborative Filtering Using Data Mining and Analysis* (pp. 250–269). Hershey, PA: IGI Global. doi:10.4018/978-1-5225-0489-4.ch014

Ogata, T. (2016). Computational and Cognitive Approaches to Narratology from the Perspective of Narrative Generation. In T. Ogata & T. Akimoto (Eds.), *Computational and Cognitive Approaches to Narratology* (pp. 1–74). Hershey, PA: IGI Global. doi:10.4018/978-1-5225-0432-0.ch001

Ozpinar, A., & Kucukasci, E. S. (2016). Use of Chaotic Randomness Numbers: Metaheuristic and Artificial Intelligence Algorithms. In N. Celebi (Ed.), *Intelligent Techniques for Data Analysis in Diverse Settings* (pp. 207–227). Hershey, PA: IGI Global. doi:10.4018/978-1-5225-0075-9.ch010

Ozpinar, A., & Ozil, E. (2016). Smart Grid and Demand Side Management: Application of Metaheuristic and Artificial Intelligence Algorithms. In A. Ahmad & N. Hassan (Eds.), *Smart Grid as a Solution for Renewable and Efficient Energy* (pp. 49–68). Hershey, PA: IGI Global. doi:10.4018/978-1-5225-0072-8.ch003

Papadopoulos, H. (2016). Designing Smart Home Environments for Unobtrusive Monitoring for Independent Living: The Use Case of USEFIL. *International Journal of E-Services and Mobile Applications*, 8(1), 47–63. doi:10.4018/IJESMA.2016010104

Papadopoulos, H. (2016). Modeling Place: Usage of Mobile Data Services and Applications within Different Places. *International Journal of E-Services and Mobile Applications*, 8(2), 1–20. doi:10.4018/IJESMA.2016040101

Parey, A., & Ahuja, A. S. (2016). Application of Artificial Intelligence to Gearbox Fault Diagnosis: A Review. In S. John (Ed.), *Handbook of Research on Generalized and Hybrid Set Structures and Applications for Soft Computing* (pp. 536–562). Hershey, PA: IGI Global. doi:10.4018/978-1-4666-9798-0.ch024

Parikh, C. (2017). Eye-Tracking Technology: A Closer Look at Eye-Tracking Paradigms with High-Risk Populations. In C. Was, F. Sansosti, & B. Morris (Eds.), *Eye-Tracking Technology Applications in Educational Research* (pp. 283–302). Hershey, PA: IGI Global. doi:10.4018/978-1-5225-1005-5.ch014

Peng, M., Qin, Y., Tang, C., & Deng, X. (2016). An E-Commerce Customer Service Robot Based on Intention Recognition Model. *Journal of Electronic Commerce in Organizations*, 14(1), 34–44. doi:10.4018/JECO.2016010104

Pessoa, C. R., & Júnior, M. D. (2017). A Telecommunications Approach in Systems for Effective Logistics and Supply Chains. In G. Jamil, A. Soares, & C. Pessoa (Eds.), *Handbook of Research on Information Management for Effective Logistics and Supply Chains* (pp. 437–452). Hershey, PA: IGI Global. doi:10.4018/978-1-5225-0973-8.ch023

Pineda, R. G. (2016). Where the Interaction Is Not: Reflections on the Philosophy of Human-Computer Interaction. *International Journal of Art, Culture and Design Technologies*, 5(1), 1–12. doi:10.4018/IJACDT.2016010101

Poitras, E. G., Harley, J. M., Compeau, T., Kee, K., & Lajoie, S. P. (2017). Augmented Reality in Informal Learning Settings: Leveraging Technology for the Love of History. In R. Zheng & M. Gardner (Eds.), *Handbook of Research on Serious Games for Educational Applications* (pp. 272–293). Hershey, PA: IGI Global. doi:10.4018/978-1-5225-0513-6.ch013

Powell, W. A., Corbett, N., & Powell, V. (2016). The Rise of the Virtual Human. In A. Connor & S. Marks (Eds.), *Creative Technologies for Multidisciplinary Applications* (pp. 99–129). Hershey, PA: IGI Global. doi:10.4018/978-1-5225-0016-2.ch005

Prakash, L. S., & Saini, D. K. (2017). Instructional Design Technology in Higher Education System: Role and Impact on Developing Creative Learning Environments. In C. Zhou (Ed.), *Handbook of Research on Creative Problem-Solving Skill Development in Higher Education* (pp. 378–406). Hershey, PA: IGI Global. doi:10.4018/978-1-5225-0643-0.ch017

Rahmani, M. E., Amine, A., & Hamou, R. M. (2016). Supervised Machine Learning for Plants Identification Based on Images of Their Leaves. *International Journal of Agricultural and Environmental Information Systems*, 7(4), 17–31. doi:10.4018/IJAEIS.2016100102

Ramanathan, U. (2017). How Smart Operations Help Better Planning and Replenishment?: Empirical Study – Supply Chain Collaboration for Smart Operations. In H. Chan, N. Subramanian, & M. Abdulrahman (Eds.), *Supply Chain Management in the Big Data Era* (pp. 25–49). Hershey, PA: IGI Global. doi:10.4018/978-1-5225-0956-1.ch003

Rao, M., & Kamila, N. K. (2017). Target Tracking in Wireless Sensor Network: The Current State of Art. In N. Kamila (Ed.), *Handbook of Research on Wireless Sensor Network Trends, Technologies, and Applications* (pp. 413–437). Hershey, PA: IGI Global. doi:10.4018/978-1-5225-0501-3.ch017

Rappaport, J. M., Richter, S. B., & Kennedy, D. T. (2016). A Strategic Perspective on Using Symbolic Transformation in STEM Education: Robotics and Automation. *International Journal of Strategic Decision Sciences*, 7(1), 39–75. doi:10.4018/IJSDS.2016010103

Rashid, E. (2016). R4 Model for Case-Based Reasoning and Its Application for Software Fault Prediction. *International Journal of Software Science and Computational Intelligence*, *8*(3), 19–38. doi:10.4018/IJSSCI.2016070102

Rathore, M. M., Paul, A., Ahmad, A., & Jeon, G. (2017). IoT-Based Big Data: From Smart City towards Next Generation Super City Planning. *International Journal on Semantic Web and Information Systems*, *13*(1), 28–47. doi:10.4018/IJSWIS.2017010103

Reeberg de Mello, A., & Stemmer, M. R. (2017). Automated Visual Inspection System for Printed Circuit Boards for Small Series Production: A Multiagent Context Approach. In O. Sergiyenko & J. Rodriguez-Quiñonez (Eds.), *Developing and Applying Optoelectronics in Machine Vision* (pp. 79–107). Hershey, PA: IGI Global. doi:10.4018/978-1-5225-0632-4.ch003

Rodrigues, P., & Rosa, P. J. (2017). Eye-Tracking as a Research Methodology in Educational Context: A Spanning Framework. In C. Was, F. Sansosti, & B. Morris (Eds.), *Eye-Tracking Technology Applications in Educational Research* (pp. 1–26). Hershey, PA: IGI Global. doi:10.4018/978-1-5225-1005-5.ch001

Rosen, Y., & Mosharraf, M. (2016). Computer Agent Technologies in Collaborative Assessments. In Y. Rosen, S. Ferrara, & M. Mosharraf (Eds.), *Handbook of Research on Technology Tools for Real-World Skill Development* (pp. 319–343). Hershey, PA: IGI Global. doi:10.4018/978-1-4666-9441-5.ch012

Rosenzweig, E. D., & Bendoly, E. (2017). An Investigation of Competitor Networks in Manufacturing Strategy and Implications for Performance. In A. Vlachvei, O. Notta, K. Karantininis, & N. Tsounis (Eds.), *Factors Affecting Firm Competitiveness and Performance in the Modern Business World* (pp. 43–82). Hershey, PA: IGI Global. doi:10.4018/978-1-5225-0843-4.ch002

S., J. R., & Omman, B. (2017). A Technical Assessment on License Plate Detection System. In M. S., & V. V. (Eds.), *Multi-Core Computer Vision and Image Processing for Intelligent Applications* (pp. 234-258). Hershey, PA: IGI Global. doi:10.4018/978-1-5225-0889-2.ch009

Saiz-Alvarez, J. M., & Leal, G. C. (2017). Cybersecurity Best Practices and Cultural Change in Global Business: Some Perspectives from the European Union. In G. Afolayan & A. Akinwale (Eds.), *Global Perspectives on Development Administration and Cultural Change* (pp. 48–73). Hershey, PA: IGI Global. doi:10.4018/978-1-5225-0629-4.ch003

Sang, Y., Zhu, Y., Zhao, H., & Tang, M. (2016). Study on an Interactive Truck Crane Simulation Platform Based on Virtual Reality Technology. *International Journal of Distance Education Technologies*, *14*(2), 64–78. doi:10.4018/IJDET.2016040105

Sarkar, D., & Roy, J. K. (2016). Artificial Neural Network (ANN) in Network Reconfiguration for Improvement of Voltage Stability. In S. Shandilya, S. Shandilya, T. Thakur, & A. Nagar (Eds.), *Handbook of Research on Emerging Technologies for Electrical Power Planning, Analysis, and Optimization* (pp. 184–206). Hershey, PA: IGI Global. doi:10.4018/978-1-4666-9911-3.ch010

Schafer, S. B. (2016). The Media-Sphere as Dream: Researching the Contextual Unconscious of Collectives. In S. Schafer (Ed.), *Exploring the Collective Unconscious in the Age of Digital Media* (pp. 232–260). Hershey, PA: IGI Global. doi:10.4018/978-1-4666-9891-8.ch010

Scheiter, K., & Eitel, A. (2017). The Use of Eye Tracking as a Research and Instructional Tool in Multimedia Learning. In C. Was, F. Sansosti, & B. Morris (Eds.), *Eye-Tracking Technology Applications in Educational Research* (pp. 143–164). Hershey, PA: IGI Global. doi:10.4018/978-1-5225-1005-5.ch008

Schneegass, S., Olsson, T., Mayer, S., & van Laerhoven, K. (2016). Mobile Interactions Augmented by Wearable Computing: A Design Space and Vision. *International Journal of Mobile Human Computer Interaction*, *8*(4), 104–114. doi:10.4018/IJMHCI.2016100106

Shah, Z., & Kolhe, A. (2017). Throughput Analysis of IEEE 802.11ac and IEEE 802.11n in a Residential Home Environment. *International Journal of Interdisciplinary Telecommunications and Networking*, *9*(1), 1–13. doi:10.4018/IJITN.2017010101

Shaqrah, A. A. (2016). Future of Smart Cities in the Knowledge-based Urban Development and the Role of Award Competitions. *International Journal of Knowledge-Based Organizations*, *6*(1), 49–59. doi:10.4018/IJKBO.2016010104

Shayan, S., Abrahamson, D., Bakker, A., Duijzer, C. A., & van der Schaaf, M. (2017). Eye-Tracking the Emergence of Attentional Anchors in a Mathematics Learning Tablet Activity. In C. Was, F. Sansosti, & B. Morris (Eds.), *Eye-Tracking Technology Applications in Educational Research* (pp. 166–194). Hershey, PA: IGI Global. doi:10.4018/978-1-5225-1005-5.ch009

Sosnin, P. I. (2017). Conceptual Experiments in Automated Designing. In R. Zuanon (Ed.), *Projective Processes and Neuroscience in Art and Design* (pp. 155–181). Hershey, PA: IGI Global. doi:10.4018/978-1-5225-0510-5.ch010

Starostenko, O., Cruz-Perez, C., Alarcon-Aquino, V., Melnik, V. I., & Tyrsa, V. (2017). Machine Vision Application on Science and Industry: Real-Time Face Sensing and Recognition in Machine Vision – Trends and New Advances. In O. Sergiyenko & J. Rodriguez-Quiñonez (Eds.), *Developing and Applying Optoelectronics in Machine Vision* (pp. 146–179). Hershey, PA: IGI Global. doi:10.4018/978-1-5225-0632-4.ch005

Stasolla, F., Boccasini, A., & Perilli, V. (2017). Assistive Technology-Based Programs to Support Adaptive Behaviors by Children with Autism Spectrum Disorders: A Literature Overview. In Y. Kats (Ed.), *Supporting the Education of Children with Autism Spectrum Disorders* (pp. 140–159). Hershey, PA: IGI Global. doi:10.4018/978-1-5225-0816-8.ch008

Stratigea, A., Leka, A., & Panagiotopoulou, M. (2017). In Search of Indicators for Assessing Smart and Sustainable Cities and Communities Performance. *International Journal of E-Planning Research*, *6*(1), 43–73. doi:10.4018/IJEPR.2017010103

Su, S., Lin, H. K., Wang, C., & Huang, Z. (2016). Multi-Modal Affective Computing Technology Design the Interaction between Computers and Human of Intelligent Tutoring Systems. *International Journal of Online Pedagogy and Course Design*, *6*(1), 13–28. doi:10.4018/IJOPCD.2016010102

Sun, X., May, A., & Wang, Q. (2017). Investigation of the Role of Mobile Personalisation at Large Sports Events. *International Journal of Mobile Human Computer Interaction*, *9*(1), 1–15. doi:10.4018/IJMHCI.2017010101

Szopa, A. (2017). The Influence of Crowdsourcing Business Model into Artificial Intelligence. In R. Batko & A. Szopa (Eds.), *Strategic Imperatives and Core Competencies in the Era of Robotics and Artificial Intelligence* (pp. 15–28). Hershey, PA: IGI Global. doi:10.4018/978-1-5225-1656-9.ch002

Tokunaga, S., Tamamizu, K., Saiki, S., Nakamura, M., & Yasuda, K. (2017). VirtualCareGiver: Personalized Smart Elderly Care. *International Journal of Software Innovation*, *5*(1), 30–43. doi:10.4018/IJSI.2017010103

Trabelsi, I., & Bouhlel, M. S. (2016). Comparison of Several Acoustic Modeling Techniques for Speech Emotion Recognition. *International Journal of Synthetic Emotions*, *7*(1), 58–68. doi:10.4018/IJSE.2016010105

Truman, B. (2017). New Constructions for Understanding using Virtual Learning-Towards Transdisciplinarity. In A. Stricker, C. Calongne, B. Truman, & F. Arenas (Eds.), *Integrating an Awareness of Selfhood and Society into Virtual Learning* (pp. 316–334). Hershey, PA: IGI Global. doi:10.4018/978-1-5225-2182-2.ch019

Turner, J. O. (2016). Virtual Soar-Agent Implementations: Examples, Issues, and Speculations. In J. Turner, M. Nixon, U. Bernardet, & S. DiPaola (Eds.), *Integrating Cognitive Architectures into Virtual Character Design* (pp. 181–212). Hershey, PA: IGI Global. doi:10.4018/978-1-5225-0454-2.ch007

Urrea, C., & Uren, V. (2017). Technical Evaluation, Development, and Implementation of a Remote Monitoring System for a Golf Cart. In N. Dey, A. Ashour, & S. Acharjee (Eds.), *Applied Video Processing in Surveillance and Monitoring Systems* (pp. 220–243). Hershey, PA: IGI Global. doi:10.4018/978-1-5225-1022-2.ch010

Veerapathiran, N., & Anand, S. (2017). Reducing False Alarms in Vision-Based Fire Detection. In N. Dey, A. Ashour, & S. Acharjee (Eds.), *Applied Video Processing in Surveillance and Monitoring Systems* (pp. 263–290). Hershey, PA: IGI Global. doi:10.4018/978-1-5225-1022-2.ch012

Vorraber, W., Lichtenegger, G., Brugger, J., Gojmerac, I., Egly, M., Panzenböck, K., & Voessner, S. et al. (2016). Designing Information Systems to Facilitate Civil-Military Cooperation in Disaster Management. *International Journal of Distributed Systems and Technologies*, 7(4), 22–40. doi:10.4018/IJDST.2016100102

Vyas, D., Kröner, A., & Nijholt, A. (2016). From Mundane to Smart: Exploring Interactions with Smart Design Objects. *International Journal of Mobile Human Computer Interaction*, 8(1), 59–82. doi:10.4018/IJMHCI.2016010103

Wang, L., Li, C., & Wu, J. (2017). The Status of Research into Intention Recognition. In J. Wu (Ed.), *Improving the Quality of Life for Dementia Patients through Progressive Detection, Treatment, and Care* (pp. 201–221). Hershey, PA: IGI Global. doi:10.4018/978-1-5225-0925-7.ch010

Wang, Y., Valipour, M., & Zatarain, O. A. (2016). Quantitative Semantic Analysis and Comprehension by Cognitive Machine Learning. *International Journal of Cognitive Informatics and Natural Intelligence*, 10(3), 13–28. doi:10.4018/IJCINI.2016070102

Xie, L., Zheng, L., & Yang, G. (2017). Hybrid Integration Technology for Wearable Sensor Systems. In C. Reis & M. Maximiano (Eds.), *Internet of Things and Advanced Application in Healthcare* (pp. 98–137). Hershey, PA: IGI Global. doi:10.4018/978-1-5225-1820-4.ch004

Xing, B., & Gao, W. (2014). Overview of Computational Intelligence. In *Computational Intelligence in Remanufacturing* (pp. 18–36). Hershey, PA: IGI Global. doi:10.4018/978-1-4666-4908-8.ch002

Xu, R., Li, Z., Cui, P., Zhu, S., & Gao, A. (2016). A Geometric Dynamic Temporal Reasoning Method with Tags for Cognitive Systems. *International Journal of Software Science and Computational Intelligence*, 8(4), 43–59. doi:10.4018/IJSSCI.2016100103

Yamaguchi, T., Nishimura, T., & Takadama, K. (2016). Awareness Based Recommendation: Passively Interactive Learning System. *International Journal of Robotics Applications and Technologies*, 4(1), 83–99. doi:10.4018/IJRAT.2016010105

Zentall, S. R., & Junglen, A. G. (2017). Investigating Mindsets and Motivation through Eye Tracking and Other Physiological Measures. In C. Was, F. Sansosti, & B. Morris (Eds.), *Eye-Tracking Technology Applications in Educational Research* (pp. 48–64). Hershey, PA: IGI Global. doi:10.4018/978-1-5225-1005-5.ch003

Zielinska, T. (2016). Professional and Personal Service Robots. *International Journal of Robotics Applications and Technologies*, 4(1), 63–82. doi:10.4018/IJRAT.2016010104

Zohora, S. E., Khan, A. M., Srivastava, A. K., Nguyen, N. G., & Dey, N. (2016). A Study of the State of the Art in Synthetic Emotional Intelligence in Affective Computing. *International Journal of Synthetic Emotions*, 7(1), 1–12. doi:10.4018/IJSE.2016010101

Index

methodology 36, 38, 41, 43, 58, 62-63, 70, 85

N

nearest neighbor 35
Neural Networks 12-14, 21, 23

P

parameters 1, 4, 7, 11, 13, 15, 42, 59, 67-69, 76-78, 81, 85, 102
perceived value 3-4
performance 3-5, 21, 36, 70
post-purchase reaction 3

Q

quality estimation 10, 12-13, 15, 30, 35-36, 58, 69, 79, 81

R

Reasoning 11-15, 19, 21-22, 24-30, 34, 36-40, 43-44, 48, 50, 53-54

S

scientific parameters 67-68
Software quality 1, 5-7, 9-15, 19, 30, 34-37, 41, 47-48, 57-59, 63, 66-70, 79, 81, 87-88, 90, 99
software quality prediction 9, 14-15, 34, 37, 47, 58
sub-branches 58

T

typical applications 19, 22

U

using machine learning 13, 35

V

validation 4, 69
verification 69

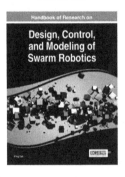

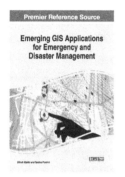